S C H O L A S T I C

LITERACY PLACE®

LAMAR UNIVERSITY LIBRARY

Acknowledgments and credits appear on pages 390–392, which constitutes an extension of this copyright page.

TABLE OF CONTENTS

Hit Series

THEME
A creative idea
can grow into
a series.

UNIT 4

TABLE OF CONTENTS

THEME
Finding information in stories and artifacts brings the past to life.

UNIT 5

TABLE OF CONTENTS

Community Quilt

THEME
In a community, some things continue and some things change.

UNIT 6

Hit Series

Hit Series

THEME

A creative idea can grow into a series.

UNIT 4

Welcome to

LITERACY PLACE

Publishing Company

A creative idea
can grow into
a series.

12

THE THREE LITTLE JAVELINAS

by **Susan Lowell**
illustrated by **Jim Harris**

This is a southwestern adaptation of a familiar folk tale: a chile-flavored "The Three Little Pigs." The story takes place in the Sonoran Desert, where Native American, Mexican, and Anglo cultures blend together.

Javelina (pronounced ha-ve-LEE-na) comes from a Spanish name for the collared peccary, a relative of swine (but not a true pig). Javelinas are extremely bristly—very hairy on the chinny-chin-chin.

13

ONCE UPON A TIME,

way out in the desert, there were three little javelinas. Javelinas (ha-ve-LEE-nas) are wild, hairy, southwestern cousins of pigs.

Their heads were hairy, their backs were hairy, and their bony legs—all the way down to their hard little hooves—were very hairy. But their snouts were soft and pink.

One day, the three little javelinas trotted away to seek their fortunes. In this hot, dry land, the sky was almost always blue. Steep purple mountains looked down on the desert, where the cactus forests grew.

Soon the little javelinas came to a spot where the path divided, and each one went a different way.

The first little javelina wandered lazily along. He didn't see a dust storm whirling across the desert—until it caught him.

The whirlwind blew away and left the first little javelina sitting in a heap of tumbleweeds. Brushing himself off, he said, "I'll build a house with them!" And in no time at all, he did.

Then along came a coyote. He ran through the desert so quickly and so quietly that he was almost invisible. In fact, this was only one of Coyote's many magical tricks. He laughed when he saw the tumbleweed house and smelled the javelina inside.

15

"Mmm! A tender juicy piggy!" he thought.
Coyote was tired of eating mice and rabbits.

He called out sweetly, "Little pig, little pig, let me come in."

"Not by the hair of my chinny-chin-chin!" shouted the first javelina (who had a lot of hair on his chinny-chin-chin!)

"Then I'll huff, and I'll puff, and I'll blow your house in!" said Coyote.

And he huffed, and he puffed, and he blew the little tumbleweed house away.

But in all the hullabaloo, the first little javelina escaped—and went looking for his brother and sister.

Coyote, who was very sneaky, tiptoed along behind.

16

The second little javelina walked for miles among giant cactus plants called saguaros (sa-WA-ros). They held their ripe red fruit high in the sky. But they made almost no shade, and the little javelina grew hot.

Then he came upon a Native American woman who was gathering sticks from inside a dried-up cactus. She planned to use these long sticks, called saguaro ribs, to knock down the sweet cactus fruit.

The second little javelina said, "Please, may I have some sticks to build a house?"

"*Ha'u*," (Ha-ou) she said, which means "yes" in the language of the Desert People.

When he was finished building his house, he lay down
in the shade. Then his brother arrived, panting from the
heat, and the second little javelina moved over and made
a place for him.

Pretty soon, Coyote found the saguaro rib house.
He used his magic to make his voice sound just like
another javelina's.

"Little pig, little pig, let me come in!" he called.

But the little javelinas were suspicious. The second
one cried, "No! Not by the hair of my chinny-chin-chin!"

"Bah!" thought Coyote. "I am not going to eat your *hair*."

Then Coyote smiled, showing all his sharp teeth: "I'll huff, and I'll puff, and I'll blow your house in!"

So he huffed, and he puffed, and all the saguaro ribs came tumbling down.

But the two little javelinas escaped into the desert.

Still not discouraged, Coyote followed. Sometimes his magic did fail, but then he usually came up with another trick.

The third little javelina trotted through beautiful palo verde trees, with green trunks and yellow flowers. She saw a snake sliding by, smooth as oil. A hawk floated round and round above her. Then she came to a place where a man was making adobe (a-DOE-be) bricks from mud and straw. The bricks lay on the ground, baking in the hot sun.

The third little javelina thought for a moment, and said, "May I please have a few adobes to build a house?"

"*Sí*," answered the man, which means "yes" in Spanish, the brick-maker's language.

So the third javelina built herself a solid little adobe house, cool in summer and warm in winter. When her brothers found her, she welcomed them in and locked the door behind them.

Coyote followed their trail.

"Little pig, little pig, let me come in!" he called.

The three little javelinas looked out the window. This time Coyote pretended to be very old and weak, with no teeth and a sore paw. But they were not fooled.

"No! Not by the hair of my chinny-chin-chin," called back the third little javelina.

"Then I'll huff, and I'll puff, and I'll blow your house in!" said Coyote. He grinned, thinking of the wild pig dinner to come.

"Just try it!" shouted the third little javelina.

So Coyote huffed and puffed, but the adobe bricks did not budge.

Again, Coyote tried. "I'LL HUFF…AND I'LL PUFF…AND I'LL BLOW YOUR HOUSE IN!"

The three little javelinas covered their hairy ears. But nothing happened. The javelinas peeked out the window.

The tip of Coyote's raggedy tail whisked right past their
noses. He was climbing upon the tin roof. Next, Coyote
used his magic to make himself very skinny.

"The stove pipe!" gasped the third little javelina.
Quickly she lighted a fire inside her wood stove.

"What a feast it will be!" Coyote said to himself.
He squeezed into the stove pipe. "I think I'll eat
them with red hot chile sauce!"

Whoosh. S-s-sizzle!

Then the three little javelinas heard an amazing noise. It was not a bark. It was not a cackle. It was not a howl. It was not a scream. It was all of those sounds together. "Yip

    yap

      yeep

        YEE-OWW-OOOOOOOOOOOOO!"

Away ran a puff of smoke shaped like a coyote.

The three little javelinas lived happily ever after in the adobe house.

And if you ever hear Coyote's voice, way out in the desert at night . . . well, you know what he's remembering!

AWARD WINNER

from Cactus Poems

SAGUARO

by Frank Asch
photographs by Ted Levin

Stand
still.
Grow
slow.
Lift
high
your arms to the sun.
Stand
still.
Grow
slow.
Lift
high
your
flowers to the sky.
Stand
still.
Grow
slow.
Hold
tight
your
water
inside.
Stand
still.
Grow
slow
and let your roots spread wide and let your roots spread wide.

THINK ABOUT READING

Answer the questions in the story map.

SETTING

1. Where does the story take place?

CHARACTERS

2. Who are the main characters in the story?

PROBLEM

3. What does the coyote want to do?

EVENTS

4. How does the coyote try to trick the javelinas?
5. What does the coyote do to the first two houses?
6. Why can't the coyote blow down the third house?

ENDING

7. Why does the coyote run away at the end of the story?

WRITE A SHAPE POEM

You, too, can write a shape poem. Picture the twirling whirlwind, the rolling tumbleweeds, the hot rays of the desert sun, and the adobe house. Choose one of these. Brainstorm describing words or phrases. Then write a poem in the shape of the thing you chose. When you're finished, draw the shape around your poem.

LITERATURE CIRCLE

What versions of "The Three Little Pigs" have you read? List them on a chart. Talk about how they are the same and how they are different. Add your ideas to the chart. Which version is your group's favorite?

AUTHOR
SUSAN LOWELL

Susan Lowell lives with her family on a small ranch in Arizona's Sonoran Desert. When she looks out her kitchen window she sometimes sees coyotes—and even javelinas. What is her favorite kind of desert plant? The giant saguaro cactus, of course!

MORE BOOKS BY SUSAN LOWELL

- *The Tortoise and the Jackrabbit*
- *The Bootmaker and the Elves*
- *I Am Lavina Cumming*
- *Little Red Cowboy Hat*

from

LITTLE HOUSE
on the
PRAIRIE

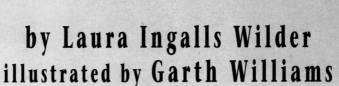

by Laura Ingalls Wilder
illustrated by Garth Williams

AWARD WINNER

The Big Woods was getting too crowded. It was time to move West. So the Ingalls family—Pa, Ma, Mary, Laura, and baby Carrie—packed their belongings into a covered wagon and hitched up the horses, Pet and Patty. With Jack, their dog, trotting under the wagon, they began the long journey to a new home on the prairie.

Many miles later, the family was glad to see a good spot for camping among some trees ahead.

et and Patty began to trot briskly, as if they were glad, too. Laura held tight to the wagon bow and stood up in the jolting wagon. Beyond Pa's shoulder and far across the waves of green grass she could see the trees, and they were not like any trees she had seen before. They were no taller than bushes.

"Whoa!" said Pa, suddenly. "Now which way?" he muttered to himself.

The road divided here, and you could not tell which was the more-traveled way. Both of them were faint wheel tracks in the grass. One went toward the west, the other sloped downward a little, toward the south. Both soon vanished in the tall, blowing grass.

"Better go downhill, I guess," Pa decided. "The creek's down in the bottoms. Must be this is the way to the ford." He turned Pet and Patty toward the south.

The road went down and up and down and up again, over gently curving land. The trees were nearer now, but they were no taller. Then Laura gasped and clutched the wagon bow, for almost under Pet's and Patty's noses there was no more blowing grass, there was no land at all. She looked beyond the edge of the land and across the tops of trees.

The road turned there. For a little way it went
along the cliff's top, then it went sharply downward.
Pa put on the brakes; Pet and Patty braced themselves
backward and almost sat down. The wagon wheels slid
onward, little by little lowering the wagon farther
down the steep slope into the ground. Jagged cliffs of
bare red earth rose up on both sides of the wagon.
Grass waved along their tops, but nothing grew on
their seamed, straight-up-and-down sides. They were
hot, and heat came from them against Laura's face.
The wind was still blowing overhead, but it did not
blow into this deep crack in the ground. The stillness
seemed strange and empty.

Then once more the wagon was level. The narrow crack down which it had come opened into the bottom lands. Here grew the tall trees whose tops Laura had seen from the prairie above. Shady groves were scattered on the rolling meadows, and in the groves deer were lying down, hardly to be seen among the shadows. The deer turned their heads toward the wagon, and curious fawns stood up to see it more clearly.

Laura was surprised because she did not see the creek. But the bottom lands were wide. Down here, below the prairie, there were gentle hills and open sunny places. The air was still and hot. Under the wagon wheels the ground was soft. In the sunny open spaces the grass grew thin, and deer had cropped it short.

For a while the high, bare cliffs of red earth stood up behind the wagon. But they were almost hidden behind hills and trees when Pet and Patty stopped to drink from the creek.

The rushing sound of the water filled the still air. All along the creek banks the trees hung over it and made it dark with shadows. In the middle it ran swiftly, sparkling silver and blue.

"This creek's pretty high," Pa said. "But I guess we can make it all right. You can see this is a ford, by the old wheel ruts. What do you say, Caroline?"

"Whatever you say, Charles," Ma answered.

Pet and Patty lifted their wet noses. They pricked their ears forward, looking at the creek; then they pricked them backward to hear what Pa would say. They sighed and laid their soft noses together to whisper to each other. A little way upstream, Jack was lapping the water with his red tongue.

STARTING OUT

Little House in the Big Woods was Laura Ingalls Wilder's first book in the series. She wrote it when she was 63 years old.

"I'll tie down the wagon-cover," Pa said. He climbed down from the seat, unrolled the canvas sides and tied them firmly to the wagon box. Then he pulled the rope at the back, so that the canvas puckered together in the middle, leaving only a tiny round hole, too small to see through.

Mary huddled down on the bed. She did not like fords; she was afraid of the rushing water. But Laura was excited; she liked the splashing. Pa climbed to the seat, saying, "They may have to swim, out there in the middle. But we'll make it all right, Caroline."

Laura thought of Jack and said, "I wish Jack could ride in the wagon, Pa."

Pa did not answer. He gathered the reins tightly in his hands. Ma said "Jack can swim, Laura. He will be all right."

The wagon went forward softly in mud. Water began to splash against the wheels. The splashing grew louder. The wagon shook as the noisy water struck at it. Then all at once the wagon lifted and balanced and swayed. It was a lovely feeling.

The noise stopped, and Ma said, sharply, "Lie down, girls!"

Quick as a flash, Mary and Laura dropped flat on the bed. When Ma spoke like that, they did as they were told. Ma's arm pulled a smothering blanket over them, heads and all.

"Be still, just as you are. Don't move!" she said.

Mary did not move; she was trembling and still.

But Laura could not help wriggling a little bit. She did so want to see what was happening. She could feel the wagon swaying and turning; the splashing was noisy again, and again it died away. Then Pa's voice frightened Laura. It said, "Take them, Caroline!"

The wagon lurched; there was a sudden heavy splash beside it. Laura sat straight up and clawed the blanket from her head.

Pa was gone. Ma sat alone, holding tight to the reins with both hands. Mary hid her face in the blanket again, but Laura rose up farther. She couldn't see the creek bank. She couldn't see anything in front of the wagon but water rushing at it. And in the water, three heads; Pet's head and Patty's head and Pa's small, wet head. Pa's fist in the water was holding tight to Pet's bridle.

Laura could faintly hear Pa's voice through the rushing of the water. It sounded calm and cheerful, but she couldn't hear what he said. He was talking to the horses. Ma's face was white and scared.

"Lie down, Laura," Ma said.

Laura lay down. She felt cold and sick. Her eyes were shut tight, but she could still see the terrible water and Pa's brown beard drowning in it.

For a long, long time the wagon swayed and swung, and Mary cried without making a sound, and Laura's stomach felt sicker and sicker. Then the front wheels struck and grated, and Pa shouted. The whole wagon jerked and jolted and tipped backward, but the wheels were turning on the ground. Laura was up again, holding to the seat; she saw Pet's and Patty's scrambling wet backs climbing a steep bank, and Pa running beside them, shouting, "Hi, Patty! Hi, Pet! Get up! Get up! Whoopsy-daisy! Good girls!"

At the top of the bank they stood still, panting and dripping. And the wagon stood still, safely out of that creek.

Pa stood panting and dripping, too, and Ma said, "Oh, Charles!"

"There, there, Caroline," said Pa. "We're all safe, thanks to a good tight wagon-box well fastened to the running-gear. I never saw a creek rise so fast in my life. Pet and Patty are good swimmers, but I guess they wouldn't have made it if I hadn't helped them."

ANOTHER HIT SERIES

The Little House books became a hit television series, too. Thousands of viewers began following the adventures of the Ingalls family in 1974.

If Pa had not known what to do, or if Ma had been too frightened to drive, or if Laura and Mary had been naughty and bothered her, then they would all have been lost. The river would have rolled them over and over and carried them away and drowned them, and nobody would ever have known what became of them. For weeks, perhaps, no other person would come along that road.

"Well," said Pa, "all's well that ends well," and Ma said, "Charles, you're wet to the skin."

Before Pa could answer, Laura cried, "Oh, where's Jack?"

They had forgotten Jack. They had left him on the other side of that dreadful water and now they could not see him anywhere. He must have tried to swim after them, but they could not see him struggling in the water now.

Laura swallowed hard, to keep from crying. She knew it was shameful to cry, but there was crying inside her. All the long way from Wisconsin poor Jack had followed them so patiently and faithfully, and now they had left him to drown. He was so tired, and they might have taken him into the wagon. He had stood on the bank and seen the wagon going away from him, as if they didn't care for him at all. And he would never know how much they wanted him.

Pa said he wouldn't have done such a thing to Jack, not for a million dollars. If he'd known how that creek would rise when they were in mid-stream, he would never have let Jack try to swim it. "But that can't be helped now," he said.

He went far up and down the creek bank, looking for Jack, calling him and whistling for him.

It was no use. Jack was gone.

Was Jack *really* swept away in the creek? Don't be kept in suspense! Read the rest of this exciting book to find out.

AWARD WINNER

FROM

SEARCHING FOR LAURA INGALLS

A Reader's Journey

by Kathryn Lasky and Meribah Knight
photographs by Christopher G. Knight

Meribah Knight loved all of Laura Ingalls Wilder's *Little House* books. And she wanted to visit Laura's many homes more than anything. One summer Meribah's wish came true. She and her family traveled by camper to some of the places Laura Ingalls had lived, including Plum Creek in western Minnesota.

In 1873 the Ingalls family had moved from Wisconsin to a dugout house that was built near Plum Creek. Laura was only six, and she couldn't swim. But she loved to wade in the creek on hot summer days and cool her toes in the clear water.

After Meribah read *On the Banks of Plum Creek*, she dreamed of swimming in the same creek where Laura had once waded. When Meribah arrived at Plum Creek, she put on an old-fashioned dress, just like one Laura once wore, and jumped in.

Here is how Meribah described Plum Creek in her diary.

◀ Meribah finds that this covered wagon, like the one Laura rode in, is very different from travel in a modern camper (above).

I finally had my dream come true, but it was almost a bad dream, a nightmare. I got to go wading and swimming in Plum Creek. ▼

It was warm and the current in the creek was going really fast. When I waded into the water I fell, but I got used to it and started to swim. When I stood up my clothes were heavy and wet. I felt like stones were hanging on my skirt. I climbed trees that were sticking out over the creek. ▶

◄ I remembered in the book how Laura went to look under branches and rocks for the old crab, the one she used to scare Nellie Oleson, the stuck-up girl in the book. I looked for it, too. I couldn't find it, so I swam along some more and hung from branches.

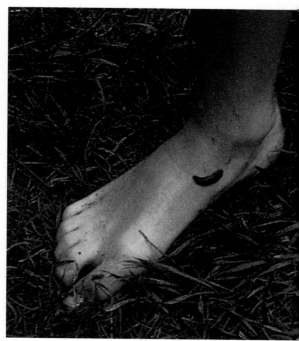

▲

But guess what? When I came out of Plum Creek I saw this thing that looked like a glob of mud on my foot, and then I thought, It's a black slug, but then I thought, Slugs aren't black. Then I remembered. It came back all awful. It was a leech just like the ones Laura got on her. I had forgotten this whole part of the book, the part about the leeches. My stomach flip-flopped, my brain went crazy, and I started to scream. Of course my dad just had to take a picture before he pulled it off me.

THINK ABOUT READING

Write your answers.

1. What happens when Laura's family tries to ford the creek?

2. What does Pa mean when he says, "Take them, Caroline!"

3. Do you agree with Pa's decision to let Jack swim across the creek? Tell why or why not.

4. How did the author make the river crossing seem real for the reader?

5. What are two ways that Meribah's story is like Laura Ingalls's story?

WRITE A STORY ENDING

Write a new ending for the story. Be sure to tell what happens to Jack. Include lots of details and tell how Laura and her family feel.

LITERATURE CIRCLE

Both Laura Ingalls and Meribah Knight travel across country. What might Laura tell Meribah about her journey? What might Meribah tell Laura?

AUTHOR
Laura Ingalls Wilder

In 1930, a 63-year-old farm woman sat down at her kitchen table to write about her pioneer childhood. That woman was Laura Ingalls Wilder. Her story grew into a series called The Little House books. To Wilder's surprise, the books became famous. Children read her stories and kept asking for more. She wrote eight books in all. Laura Ingalls Wilder died in 1957 at the age of 90, but her story lives on in her popular books.

More Books by
Laura Ingalls Wilder

- *On the Banks of Plum Creek*
- *By the Shores of Silver Lake*
- *The Long Winter*

How to
Write a Series Review

author of
the series

How did you discover your favorite hit series? Did a friend tell you about it? Did you read a glowing review about it in a newspaper or magazine?

a favorite
scene

What is a review? A review is one person's opinion about a book, movie, cartoon, comic book, TV show, video game, or some other kind of entertainment.

how the
reviewer
feels about
the book

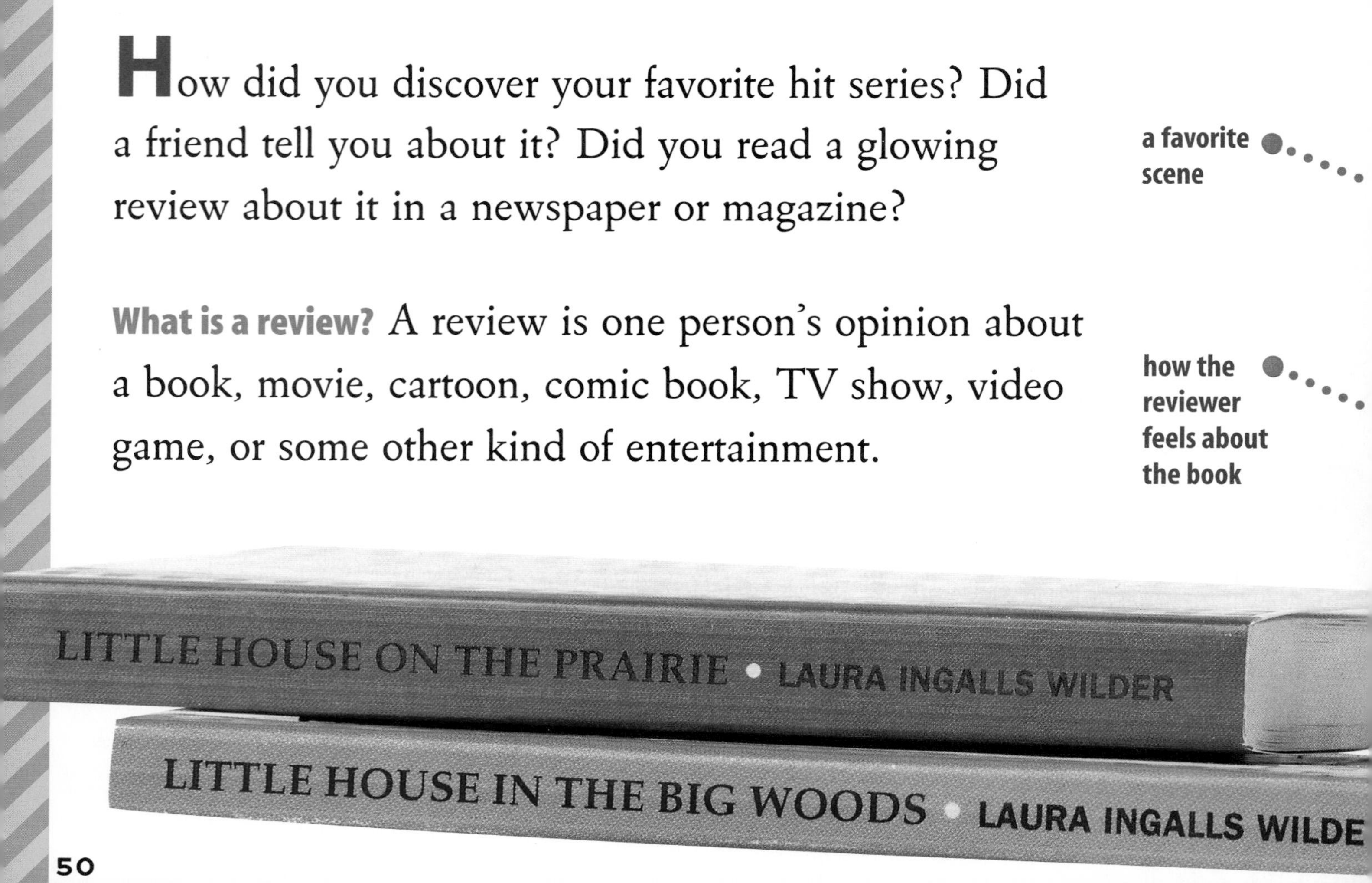

LITTLE HOUSE ON THE PRAIRIE • LAURA INGALLS WILDER

LITTLE HOUSE IN THE BIG WOODS • LAURA INGALLS WILDE

name of reviewer

title of the review names one book in the series

where and when the story takes place

ANTWON BUTLER

age 8

LITTLE HOUSE IN THE BIG WOODS

Laura Ingalls Wilder is the author of *Little House in the Big Woods* and also its main character. This first book in the Little House series is about the Ingalls family, who lived in a cabin in northern Wisconsin a long time ago. I especially liked one chapter called "Dance at Grandpa's." Grandma dances and even beats Uncle George in a dance called a jig. I could picture that in my mind, and it made me laugh. The book also tells you how to make maple syrup.

When I finished reading this book, I was sad it was over. So I read the rest of the series. I think people should read these books because you find out that even though Laura lived many years ago she was still a kid, and kids will always have things in common.

ILLUSTRATED BY GARTH WILLIAMS

1 Choose a Series

Choose a series to review. If you can't think of a series, ask a friend, teacher, or librarian to suggest a good one. Then gather several books, cartoons, or comics in the series. If you are reviewing a TV or movie series, jot down the titles of some episodes you have seen.

TOOLS

• pencil and paper

2 Make Notes

Make some notes about the series you have chosen. Here are some questions to help you:

• Is it a series you read or one that you watch?

• Is the series fiction or nonfiction? If it's fiction, what kind of story is it? If it's nonfiction, what topic does it tell about?

• What's the same in each book or episode? What's different?

• Who are your favorite characters? Why?

• Which book or episode do you want to review?

3 Write Your Review

Use your notes to write your review. Include the title of the episode, the series it came from, and the author. Tell what the series is about. Don't forget to describe an important scene from one episode. Be sure to tell your readers how you feel about the series. Last, but not least, sign your review, so everyone will know who wrote it.

4 Share Your Review

Read your review aloud to your classmates, and answer any questions they have. For anyone who is interested, you can suggest other favorite books or episodes in the series.

If You Are Using a Computer ...

Write your review in the Newsletter format. Create a headline. Use clip art so your review looks like a newspaper article.

Tip How do you rate the series you just reviewed? Was it fantastic, great, good, or just okay? Write your rating at the top of your review.

THINK

Reviewers tell their opinions about books, TV, movies, and music. Why do you think it's important to read these reviews?

Joanna Cole and
Bruce Degen
Author and Illustrator ▶

Scholastic's

TELEVISION SCRIPT

AWARD WINNER

Scholastic's

from

The Magic School Bus
Hops Home

a TV Script by Jocelyn Stevenson

illustrated by **Nancy Stevenson**

based on **The Magic School Bus®** book series

by **JOANNA COLE** and **BRUCE DEGEN**

FROM THE DESK OF MS. FRIZZLE

Time for another adventure on The Magic School Bus!

This week, we're studying habitats—the places where animals live. Wanda wanted to do her part, so she brought her bullfrog Bella to school. Wanda tried to make a perfect classroom habitat for Bella, but Bella had other ideas. When Arnold opened a window, Bella hopped out!

Ms.Frizzle

Wanda

Dorothy Ann

Keesha

Phoebe

Arnold

Tim

Ralphie

Carlos

Liz the Lizard

THE MAGIC SCHOOL BUS
HOPS HOME

CHARACTERS

WANDA	PHOEBE
ARNOLD	KEESHA
RALPHIE	CARLOS
TIM	DOROTHY ANN
MS. FRIZZLE	LIZ THE LIZARD

[INTERIOR OF MS. FRIZZLE'S CLASSROOM. DAYTIME.]

WANDA

Arnold!! Bella's gone!!!

ARNOLD

Gone? Where?

WANDA

Out the window! Arnold, did you
open it?

ARNOLD

[shakes his head innocently] Well yes,
but—I thought she could use some
air.

[Everyone runs to the window to look out. RALPHIE comes
up to ARNOLD.]

RALPHIE

Nice one, Arnold.

[WANDA wanders grief–stricken around the room.]

WANDA

Why would Bella leave? Why? Why? Why? It's so perfect here!

[TIM holds up the duck mug in one hand and the beanbag frog in the other.]

TIM

Maybe she needed more from her habitat than a duck mug and a beanbag shaped like a frog …

[WANDA takes the mug and beanbag away from TIM and puts them with all of Bella's other toys.]

WANDA

Tim, those were her special things!

[WANDA faces everyone.]

WANDA

I've got to find her!

[Then she grabs ARNOLD, who's trying to sneak back to his desk.]

WANDA

And you've got to help me.

[She grabs the beanbag frog.]

WANDA

Ms. Frizzle? Could we be excused to go look for Bella?

[MS. FRIZZLE raises an eyebrow at LIZ, who starts to pack up her hammock.]

MS. FRIZZLE

That's an excellent idea, Wanda! In fact …

CUT TO means to quickly change from one scene to another.

[MS. FRIZZLE'S dragonfly earrings start to spin.]

MS. FRIZZLE

… why don't we make it a …

[The kids run for the door.]

ARNOLD

Oh no!

KIDS

Field trip!!!

[CUT TO: INTERIOR OF MAGIC SCHOOL BUS. DAYTIME. MS. FRIZZLE is at the wheel. WANDA sits right behind her, clutching her beanbag frog, worrying. LIZ is stringing up her hammock. ARNOLD climbs on the bus and takes a seat.]

ARNOLD

I think I should have stayed home today.

WANDA

I think Bella should have stayed home today! How are we ever going to find her? She could have hopped anywhere!

MS. FRIZZLE

Not exactly anywhere, Wanda. As I always say, to find a frog, be a frog.

[MS. FRIZZLE starts pushing buttons on the dashboard.]

ARNOLD

Be a frog?!! Oh no! Does that
mean we're going to …

[CUT TO: EXTERIOR OF MAGIC SCHOOL BUS.
Through some funny changes, it shrinks to the size of a
very large bullfrog—complete with frogs' legs. Now it is
a bus/frog.]

ARNOLD

… shrink …

[The BUS/FROG hops past an amazed cat, toward rear of
school, and out of frame.]

KIDS

[OFF] Whoooaaaaaaaaahhhhhh!!!

[CUT TO: INTERIOR OF BUS/FROG.
The kids look as if they're riding a bucking bronco,
and RALPHIE doesn't like it.]

RALPHIE

Hey, take it easy.

[LIZ is hanging onto her hammock for dear life. WANDA
and ARNOLD peer anxiously out the window, as the
landscape rises and falls with each hop. MS. FRIZZLE
sings to herself, happy as a clam.]

MS. FRIZZLE

[humming] "Where oh where has
my little frog gone. …"

[WANDA leans forward—suddenly excited!]

WANDA

Ms. Frizzle, maybe Bella just
hopped out to find some food!

SHOT OF means a picture taken by the camera.

[SHOT OF RALPHIE who dizzily watches the landscape go by.]

RALPHIE

Food? Who can think of food at a time like this?

[SHOT OF MS. FRIZZLE, who smiles.]

MS. FRIZZLE

That is definitely a speculation worth consideration, Wanda!

ARNOLD

What kind of food? Cornflakes? Malloblasters?

WANDA

Bugs!

PHOEBE

[gasps] Eeww!!

[SHOT OF KEESHA, who's enjoying this.]

KEESHA

Maybe we should hop to the nearest bug habitat to have a look!

MS. FRIZZLE

What do you say, class?

[SHOT OF RALPHIE clutching his stomach.]

RALPHIE

Uh, Ms. Frizzle, do we have to hop?

[EXTERIOR. CLEARING.
We see a clearing complete with birds, a dead log, a few trees, and low growing plants and bushes. BUS/FROG hops into frame, landing beside log. BUS/FROG stops and the door opens.]

MS. FRIZZLE

Everybody out!

[SHOT OF the kids who slowly climb out of BUS/FROG and look around. LIZ stumbles out, dragging her hammock behind her. WANDA pushes past.]

WANDA

[calling] Bella! Bella! Where are you?? Belllaaaaaahhhh!!!

[ARNOLD cringes from the volume of her voice.]

ARNOLD

Wanda! Quiet! You'll scare her away!

WANDA

[frustrated] Thanks to you, she's already away, Arnold. The question is where!

[Before another argument can start, a very big grasshopper hops by. MS. FRIZZLE scoops LIZ (with hammock) up into her arms and hops onto the grasshopper's back.]

MS. FRIZZLE

Hop along, class! Two by two, please!!

[Kids hop after MS. FRIZZLE, all except for RALPHIE, who's still feeling a little ill.]

A WIDE SHOT is a picture that shows a wide area.

RALPHIE

Thanks, but I'll wa-a-alk!!!

[A beetle scuttles between RALPHIE'S legs, taking him with it.]

RALPHIE

Whoa!!

[WIDE SHOT. Top of the log. MS. FRIZZLE and LIZ get off their grasshopper. The kids scramble up after her, dodging bugs. The place is crawling with them!]

CARLOS

Hey, this place is crawling with frog food!

[RALPHIE gets dumped by his beetle.]

RALPHIE

Oooff! [moans] Do you have to keep talking about food?

[MS. FRIZZLE helps him up.]

MS. FRIZZLE

Sorry, Ralphie, but food is one of the things all plants and animals need from their habitat.

[WANDA bears down on ARNOLD.]

WANDA

So, here's the food, Arnold. Where's Bella?

[ARNOLD lifts up leaves, fungi, moss looking for BELLA.]

ARNOLD

I'm looking ... I'm looking.

SFX means sound effects.

[He parts some leaves on a branch and finds himself face to face with a cat.]
[SFX: CAT'S MEOW.]

ARNOLD

Yikes! I'm running!

[SHOT OF MS. FRIZZLE as she walks over to the cat.]

MS. FRIZZLE

[delighted] Oh look! It's a Felis Catus!

[BUS/FROG hops into frame and kids make a mad dash into it.]

KIDS

Hurry, hurry! Go, go! Let's get out of here!

[MS. FRIZZLE strolls back to BUS/FROG as the cat looks at her, confused.]

MS. FRIZZLE

But this is an excellent opportunity to study the behavior of cats!

KIDS

Ms. Frizzle!!

[CUT TO: INTERIOR OF BUS/FROG. DAYTIME.
MS. FRIZZLE steps into BUS/FROG and sits down and closes the bus door. She punches a button or throws a lever.]

MS. FRIZZLE

Here we go!

[CUT TO: EXTERIOR OF BUS/FROG.
The cat pounces, but BUS/FROG shoots up and out of the frame just in time.]

MS. FRIZZLE

[OFF] Waaaahooooooooooooo!!!

[BUS/FROG lands in a tree.]
[CUT TO: INTERIOR OF BUS/FROG.
WANDA looks out window. She can't believe it.]

WANDA

We're in a tree??!?

[CARLOS tries to comfort her.]

CARLOS

Don't worry, Wanda. It's just a little mis-hop.

ALL KIDS

Carlos!

[The kids look out and find themselves staring at a squirrel family, which stares back. LIZ comes out from under the seat and takes a look.]

MS. FRIZZLE

Not a mis-hop, Carlos. A tree is a wonderful habitat!

[She takes them all off BUS/FROG.]
[CUT TO: EXTERIOR OF BUS/FROG. DAYTIME.
BUS/FROG is parked dangerously next to a hole in the tree where some squirrels have made their nest. The kids balance uncertainly on the branches. We see the cat stalking down below.]

DOROTHY ANN

According to my research, it is a perfect place for squirrels and birds!

[Bird tweets and flies by. Squirrels scamper down the trees.]

KEESHA

[looking down at cat] Yeah, it gives them a safe place away from cats to build their nests.

[One of the squirrels moves to reveal baby squirrels.]

PHOEBE

Oh look! Baby squirrels!

[WANDA is bursting with frustration.]

WANDA

But I don't want baby squirrels! I want Bella. And there's not enough space for her here. There's no food. Besides, where would she put her swimming pool?

[RALPHIE points to a limb of the tree.]

RALPHIE

I don't know. How about over there?

WANDA

Very funny, Ralphie.

[She looks up. Grabbing ARNOLD, she starts to climb.]

WANDA

Come on, Arnold. Let's see if we can see her.

ARNOLD

[hesitating] But Wanda …

[SFX: CREAKING BRANCH.]
[WANDA suddenly sees something below hopping away. Is it a frog?]

WANDA

There she is! Look! Bella! Bellllaaahh!

[She pulls ARNOLD after her.]

ARNOLD

No wait—Wanda!

WANDA

Bella!

ARNOLD

Wanda, wait! Be careful! Wanda!

[WANDA falls off the branch, pulling ARNOLD with her. At the last second, he grabs onto a twig, stopping them from falling. They hang there. ARNOLD dangles from the twig and WANDA holds onto ARNOLD'S foot.]

ARNOLD

What do we do now, Wanda?

[They look down— see cat looking up hungrily—look at each other...]

WANDA AND ARNOLD

Heeeeellllppp!!!

[SFX: CREAKING BRANCH AS A CREATURE JUMPS OFF.]

[WIDEN to include the hopping creature that caught CAT's eye. It lands in front of CAT down below. It's a praying mantis.]

ARNOLD

[through clenched teeth] That wasn't Bella, Wanda!

WANDA

So? I knew that!

ARNOLD

Then WHY ARE WE HERE??!?

[SFX: BEEP! BEEP! OF BUS/FROG.]

[SHOT OF BUS/FROG hopping onto a branch below ARNOLD and WANDA. Its roof opens and a large funnel emerges. A cheerful and relaxed MS. FRIZZLE is at the wheel and calls through a bullhorn.]

MS. FRIZZLE

Wanda? Arnold? Come along now! I can't have you two hanging out here all day!

[ARNOLD and WANDA let go and BUS/FROG catches them. BUS/FROG closes its "eyes," leaps off the branch, lands on the ground, and hops away.]

RALPHIE

Here we go again!

FROM THE DESK OF MS. FRIZZLE

We followed Bella's trail to a quiet pond and found her sitting on a lily pad. Wanda realized that the pond was a perfect home for Bella, so she tearfully said goodbye. Back in our classroom, Wanda had a real case of the bullfrog blues. But Wanda's sad tale has a "hoppy" ending. We made Wanda a giant paper frog to cheer her up. And that frog's habitat is the classroom.

THE END

THE VOICES BEHIND THE SCENES

MALCOLM-JAMAL WARNER

If the Producer, who often appears at the end of each episode, sounds familiar, it's no wonder! You're hearing the voice of **Malcolm-Jamal Warner.** The actor played Theo on the popular TV comedy, *The Cosby Show.*

LILY TOMLIN

Actress **Lily Tomlin** was perfect for the voice of Ms. Frizzle. After experimenting with many different voices, Tomlin found one that seemed just right—chirpy and cheerful! She won an Emmy for her portrayal.

LITTLE RICHARD

Famous rock 'n' roll star **Little Richard** sings *The Magic School Bus* theme song. His hits include a rock 'n' roll version of "Itsy Bitsy Spider."

LISA YAMANAKA

The voice of Wanda is recorded by **Lisa Yamanaka**. She can also be heard in two other animated TV series, *Little Rosey* and *Family Dog.*

69

MENTORS

Joanna Cole & Bruce Degen

Author and Illustrator

Creating books is more fun than riding a roller coaster!

Who really drives the Magic School Bus? Did you say Ms. Frizzle? Well, think again. The brains behind the wheel are Joanna Cole and Bruce Degen. Together they create this exciting series.

PROFILE

Names: Joanna Cole, Bruce Degen

Job:
Cole: author
Degen: illustrator

Former jobs:
Cole: baby-sitter, TV factory worker, editor
Degen: opera-scenery painter, art teacher

Favorite school subjects:
Cole: science
Degen: art and reading

First published books:
Cole: Cockroaches
Degen: Aunt Possum and the Pumpkin Man

Where you'd like to go on the Magic School Bus:
Cole: inside the human body
Degen: the South Seas

71

UESTIONS
for Joanna Cole and Bruce Degen, Author and Illustrator

Here's how author Joanna Cole and illustrator Bruce Degen create a hit series.

 How did The Magic School Bus books come about?

A *Cole:* I had been writing children's science books for about 15 years when I began the Magic School Bus series. The idea was a teacher who loves science would take her class on trips where no kids had ever gone before.

Q **How do you decide what to write about?**

A *Degen:* We brainstorm together. Once, on a cross-country plane trip, we came up with a list of 40 possible topics for our books!

 What's it like working together on a series?

A *Cole:* Bruce and I make a good team! I research and write the book.
Degen: Then I come up with illustrations that go with the text. We have many meetings to figure out exactly what words and pictures go on every page.

Q **Was Ms. Frizzle inspired by a real person?**

A *Cole:* Oh, yes. I had a science teacher who was just like Ms. Frizzle—she was so enthusiastic about science! Ms. Frizzle is also a lot like me. I like to explain science to kids.

Q **How did you decide what to make Ms. Frizzle look like?**

A *Degen:* I pictured my high school teachers, who often wore simple dresses. To make Ms. Frizzle look distinctive, I added outrageous patterns.

Q **What about Arnold?**

A *Cole:* Arnold likes to stay at home—he's the opposite of Ms. Frizzle!

Q **What's the best thing about working on this series?**

A *Degen:* It's exciting!
Cole: We're always learning something new.

Joanna Cole and Bruce Degen's Tips to Young Writers

1 Think of an interesting topic or story. Research it.

2 Plan what you're going to write. Make sketches.

3 Put the text and art together to make a book.

73

Think About Reading

Write your answers.

1. Where does the Magic School Bus take Ms. Frizzle's class? Why?

2. What is unusual about Ms. Frizzle's school bus in this story?

3. Would you like to have Ms. Frizzle as your teacher? Tell why or why not.

4. What special features does a TV script have?

5. How is author Joanna Cole like Ms. Frizzle?

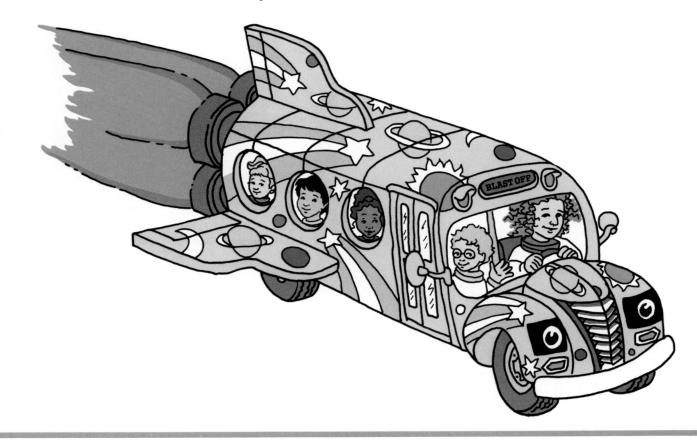

Write a Home Page Biography

Imagine that Ms. Frizzle has a site on the Internet. Write a short biography about her that will appear on her home page. Tell what she looks like and what she does. Include the titles of books and TV shows in which she has starred.

Literature Circle

Bruce Degen and Joanna Cole made a list of 40 possible topics for their Magic School Bus books. Talk about field trips you would like to take on the Magic School Bus. Discuss where you would go and what you would like to find out. Make a list of the places. Then choose the top three.

Author and Illustrator
Joanna Cole and Bruce Degen

Joanna Cole always asks herself this question as she writes a Magic School Bus book. "Why does the reader want to turn the page?" Her goal is to make the book so interesting that students can't stop reading.

Bruce Degen keeps readers interested with his clever and funny drawings. He often gets ideas for his Magic School Bus illustrations from magazine photographs.

More Books by
Cole and Degen

- *The Magic School Bus Inside a Hurricane*
- *The Magic School Bus Inside a Beehive*

MYSTERY

from
ENCYCLOPEDIA BROWN
LENDS A HAND

THE

CASE *of the*

RUNAWAY

ELEPHANT

AWARD WINNER

by Donald J. Sobol

illustrated by Leonard Shortall

cross the length and breadth of America people were wondering:

"What is Idaville's secret?"

For more than a year now, no one had gotten away with a crime in Idaville.

Aside from being a model of law and order, Idaville was a lovely seaside town. It had clean beaches and three movie theaters. It had churches, a synagogue, four banks, and two delicatessens.

The chief of police was Mr. Brown. He knew that nearly every American thought he was the best peace officer in the nation. He also knew the truth about Idaville.

The real brains behind Idaville's war on crime was his only child, ten-year-old Encyclopedia.

Whenever Chief Brown had a mystery he could not solve, he put his emergency plan into action. He went home to dinner. At the table he told Encyclopedia the facts.

The boy detective solved the case before dessert. Once in a while, however, he had to ask for second helpings to gain more time.

Chief Brown hated keeping his son's ability a secret. He felt Congress should award Encyclopedia a vote of thanks. But how could he suggest it?

Who would believe that the guiding hand behind Idaville's police record could make a yo-yo loop-the-loop off a man-on-the-flying trapeze?

"Mr. Hunt opened his eyes, and there was Jimbo peeping through the window."

No one.

So Chief Brown said nothing.

Encyclopedia never let slip a word about the help he gave his father. He did not want to seem different from other fifth-graders.

But he was stuck with his nickname.

Only his parents and teachers called him by his right name, Leroy. Everyone else in Idaville called him Encyclopedia.

An encyclopedia is a book or set of books filled with facts from A to Z. Encyclopedia had read so many books he was really more like a library. You might say he was the only library in which the information desk was on the top floor.

One evening Chief Brown looked up from his soup. "Friday the thirteenth," he muttered.

"You're mistaken, dear," said Mrs. Brown. "Today is Friday the twelfth."

"I'm talking about seventeen years ago," said Chief Brown.

"Does the date have something to do with a case?" asked Encyclopedia.

"Yes, with Mr. Hunt's elephant, Jimbo," answered Chief Brown. "The animal is causing a problem."

Encyclopedia refused to believe his ears. Jimbo was the only pet elephant in Idaville. He never caused anyone a problem. Mr. Hunt kept him in the backyard.

"If Jimbo is in the middle of a mystery, tell Leroy," urged Mrs. Brown. "It could be his biggest case."

Chief Brown nodded. "It turns out that Jimbo may not belong to Mr. Hunt after all," he began. "Mr. Hunt found him outside his bedroom window on April Fools' Day seventeen years ago."

"What a shock for him!" exclaimed Mrs. Brown.

"I imagine so," replied Chief Brown. "Mr. Hunt opened his eyes, and there was Jimbo peeping through the window. He woke up Mrs. Hunt to make sure he wasn't dreaming."

"What did she say?" asked Encyclopedia.

" 'I hope he's on a leash,' " replied Chief Brown, "according to Mr. Hunt."

"Mr. Hunt has a great memory," marveled Encyclopedia.

"So does Mr. Xippas," said Chief Brown. "He came to my office today. He says he owns the elephant and wants him back. He claims Mr. Hunt never paid for Jimbo."

"What does Mr. Hunt say?" inquired Mrs. Brown.

"Mr. Hunt insists that he mailed the money to Mr. Xippas," said Chief Brown.

He waited while Mrs. Brown cleared the soup bowls. When she had served the ham loaf, he took his notebook from his breast pocket.

"I spoke with both Mr. Xippas and Mr. Hunt today," he said. "I'll give you Mr. Hunt's side first."

Encyclopedia and his mother listened as Chief Brown read from his notes.

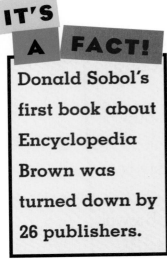

IT'S A FACT!

Donald Sobol's first book about Encyclopedia Brown was turned down by 26 publishers.

"Mr. Hunt says that he thought the elephant in his backyard was a prank, since it was April Fools' Day. He immediately called the police. It turned out that the elephant had run away from a little circus which had just arrived in town.

"An hour later Mr. Xippas came to Mr. Hunt's house. Mr. Xippas owned and trained Jimbo. By then the Hunts had taken a liking to the animal. They asked Mr. Xippas if he would sell him.

"Mr. Xippas agreed. He also agreed to stay at the Hunts' house a week or two. The couple wanted to learn how to care for Jimbo. Mr. Xippas, however, asked to see their money first. So that afternoon Mr. Hunt drew the cash from the Oceanside Bank and showed it to the animal trainer.

"After nearly two weeks, the Hunts felt they could handle the friendly Jimbo. Mr. Hunt offered Mr. Xippas the money. Mr. Xippas wouldn't take it because it was Friday the thirteenth, which he said was bad luck for him.

"The same night Mr. Xippas left Idaville. He left a forwarding address, and Mr. Hunt mailed him the money."

Chief Brown looked up from his notebook.

"That's Mr. Hunt's story," he said. "Mr. Xippas insists he never got the money. The address was his sister's house in New Jersey. He says she was sick and had telephoned him to come and be with her."

"Why did Mr. Xippas wait seventeen years before coming back to Idaville to claim Jimbo?" asked Encyclopedia. "It doesn't sound right."

"He says his sister died shortly after he reached her bedside," replied Chief Brown. "A day after her death, he got an offer of a job in India. He's been overseas all this time. He only returned to the United States five days ago."

"I wonder about him," said Mrs. Brown. "Why did he ask to see Mr. Hunt's money that very first day? I don't think that was nice. He should have trusted Mr. Hunt."

"Mr. Xippas says he didn't ask to see the money," answered Chief Brown. "He says Mr. Hunt never went to the bank. Furthermore, the only reason he stayed so long with the Hunts was that every day Mr. Hunt promised to pay him the following day."

Chief Brown closed his notebook.

"I should add," he said, "that Mr. Xippas denies that he refused the money on Friday the thirteenth because it was bad luck. He says the only thing Mr. Hunt gave him were promises to pay."

"What about the bank?" said Mrs. Brown. "Don't banks keep records?"

"A hurricane struck later that year," said Chief Brown. "It flooded the Oceanside Bank, Mr. Hunt's home, and most of the buildings in Idaville. All the records were destroyed."

"I still don't understand something," said Mrs. Brown. "Mr. Xippas worked in the circus. How could he take nearly two weeks off to stay with the Hunts?"

"Mr. Xippas told me that he had become tired of circus life," said Chief Brown. "By selling Jimbo, he could quit and open his own business."

"Whom to believe?" sighed Mrs. Brown.

She had risen to clear the dishes and bring in the dessert. She glanced at Encyclopedia with concern. He always solved a case before dessert. Was this case too hard?

The boy detective closed his eyes. He always closed his eyes when he did his deepest thinking.

Suddenly his eyes opened. "Dad," he said. "Both men have memories like an elephant. But the one who is lying is Mr.——"

WHO?

Turn the page

for the

solution *to*

the case.

SOLUTION TO
THE
CASE *of the*
RUNAWAY
ELEPHANT

Mr. Hunt never paid for the elephant.

He lied when he said Mr. Xippas refused to accept payment on Friday the thirteenth because it was bad luck.

But what tripped him up was another lie. He said he had gone to the bank on April Fools' Day and had drawn out the money to buy Jimbo. Impossible!

Because it happened seventeen years ago, he thought he was safe. He had not reckoned on Encyclopedia.

April Fools' Day is April 1.

As Encyclopedia knew, if in any month a Friday falls on the thirteenth, the first day of the month is Sunday.

On Sundays banks are closed.

from

101

Elephant
JokeS

Compiled by **ROBERT BLAKE**

Illustrated by **PETER SPACEK**

Why are elephants trumpeters?

It is too hard for them to learn to play the piano!

Why do elephants wear blue sneakers?

Their red ones are in the laundry!

Why do elephants wear sneakers while jumping from tree to tree?

They don't want to wake up the neighbors!

What time is it when an elephant sits on a fence?

Time to buy a new fence!

What's gray and white and red all over?

An embarrassed elephant!

Where do you find elephants?

It depends on where you leave them!

from

I SPY

Photographs by Walter Wick
Riddles by Jean Marzollo

I spy a shovel, a long silver chain,
A little toy horse, a track for a train;

A birthday candle, a pretty gold ring,
A small puzzle piece, and a crown for a king.

I spy a turtle, a penny for a wish,
A door ajar, and a jewelry fish;

Four anchors, a ship, a shadowy whale,
A pot of gold, and A MERMAID'S TALE.

THE MAKING OF I SPY

It takes a quick mind and a sharp eye,
To bring you the series that's known as I SPY!

Jean Marzollo and Walter Wick put their talents together in the eye-catching *I SPY* series.

Getting Started

Each book begins with Jean Marzollo and Walter Wick discussing a theme and brainstorming ideas for the photos. Then Wick goes looking for objects for the photographs.

The number of items needed for each photo is mind-boggling! Wick's search takes him to flea markets, crafts shops, toy stores, and even friends' attics.

Wick sets up the shot.

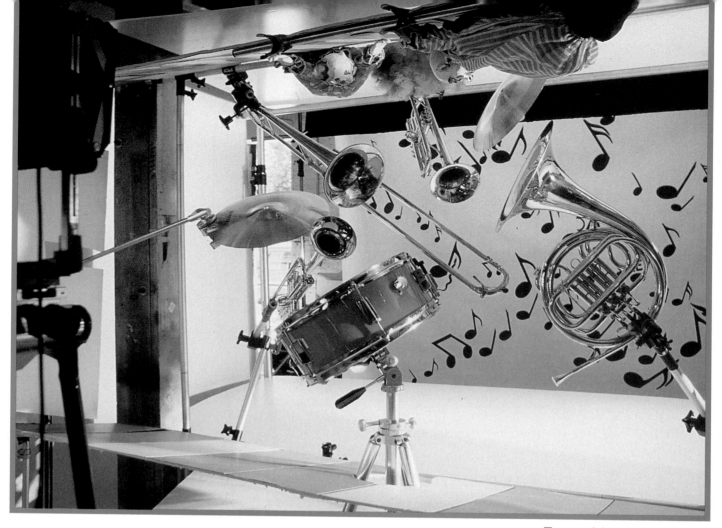

Everything is in place.

Shooting *I SPY*

To create one of the photographs for *I SPY Fun House,* Wick first built a wooden frame. From it he hung shiny musical instruments. Next he glued cut-out musical notes onto a white wall. Special lights made the wall look blue.

Wick placed colorful toy clowns above the instruments so they would be reflected in the horns. It took several days for everything to look just right. When it did, Wick shot the picture. Lights! Camera! Click!

This is "Circus Band," one of the photos that appeared in *I SPY Fun House.*

91

THINK About Reading

Answer the questions in the story map.

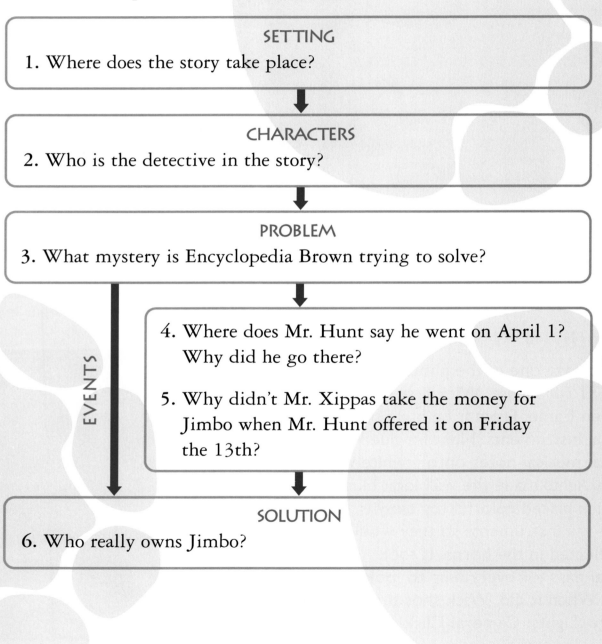

SETTING

1. Where does the story take place?

CHARACTERS

2. Who is the detective in the story?

PROBLEM

3. What mystery is Encyclopedia Brown trying to solve?

EVENTS

4. Where does Mr. Hunt say he went on April 1? Why did he go there?

5. Why didn't Mr. Xippas take the money for Jimbo when Mr. Hunt offered it on Friday the 13th?

SOLUTION

6. Who really owns Jimbo?

Write About What Happens Next

What happens to the elephant Jimbo after the story ends? Does he stay with Mr. Hunt or return to his old trainer, Mr. Xippas? Write a paragraph in which you describe what happens next to Jimbo.

Literature Circle

A mystery and a picture riddle are both puzzles. Imagine you could talk to mystery author Donald Sobol and the creators of *I Spy*—Walter Wick and Jean Marzollo. What questions would you ask them about the "puzzles" they wrote? What answers might they give you? Make a list of the questions and possible answers.

Author Donald Sobol

The idea for the character of Encyclopedia Brown came to Donald Sobol over thirty years ago. Sobol has been writing books about everyone's favorite boy detective ever since. He's proud that his books offer both challenging mysteries and lots of laughs. The author says, "Encyclopedia is the kid I wanted to be when I was ten years old!"

More Books by DONALD SOBOL

- *Encyclopedia Brown and the Case of the Treasure Hunt*
- *Encyclopedia Brown and the Case of the Disgusting Sneakers*
- *Still More Two-Minute Mysteries*

How to
Make a Character Fact File

the series in
which the
character
appears ● . . . .

the character's
name ● . . . .

age ● . . . .

what the ● . . . .
character
looks like

Authors of hit series have fantastic imaginations! They create characters that appear in books, TV series, comics, or even video games. How do series authors keep track of the characters they create? One way is to make a fact file for each character.

What is a character fact file? A character fact file tells important details about a character.

SERIES:
The Baby-sitters Club

CHARACTER:
Jackie Rodowsky

facts about the character's family

- seven years old
- red hair, red cheeks, freckles
- big grin, with one tooth missing
- has two brothers, Shea and Archie
- loses tooth playing ball; likes losing teeth
- hits a home run and breaks the window of his elementary school
- baby-sitter, Jessi, helps him make a working volcano for the science fair; but she does most of the work
- is called the "walking disaster"
- is accident-prone
- plays the kazoo in a band that the Baby-sitters Club organizes
- has a pet grasshopper named Elizabeth

important events in the character's life

other details about the character

1 | Create a Character

Think of a hit series you like. Then make up a new character who can appear in the series. You might create a new superhero, a girl detective who helps Encyclopedia Brown, a new neighbor for Charlie Brown, a cat who helps Lassie, or a new friend for Ramona Quimby. There are hundreds of series in need of new characters.

TOOLS

- pencil and paper
- colored pencils or marking pens

Tips
- A character can be like someone you know.
- A character can have special talents—jumping rope, leaping tall buildings, or being a computer whiz.
- A character can do unusual things—a pig who can fly, or a boy who can see in the dark.

2 | List Character Facts

What is your character like? These questions can help you think of details about your character. Jot down your ideas.

- In which series will this character appear?
- What is the character's name?
- What does the character look like?
- Where does the character live?
- What hobbies does the character have?
- Is the character funny, serious, friendly, helpful, or playful?

Angela the Detective

The Robot Roberto

3 Make a Fact File

Now you can make a character fact file. At the top of a sheet of paper, write the character's name. Below the name, write all the information you have made up about the character. Be sure to include the series in which the character will appear. If you wish, draw a picture of your character on a separate sheet of paper. Put it with the character's fact file.

4 Discuss Your Character

You have written down a lot of information about the character you created. Now let your classmates read your character fact file. Answer questions about the character. Compare the character to the ones your classmates have created. Will any of the characters appear in the same series?

If You Are Using a Computer ...

You can use your Journal format to write about your character on your computer, too. Use clip art to show what your character looks like.

THINK
Writers often put bits of themselves into characters. How is the character that you just created similar to or different from the real you?

Joanna Cole and
Bruce Degen
Author and Illustrator ▶

AWARD WINNER

from

THE BABY SITTERS CLUB

Jessi's Baby-sitter

by Ann M. Martin

illustrated by Scott Ernster

Baby-sitters Club Notebook

Wednesday

Well, here we go again. Another afternoon with Jackie Rodowsky, the walking disaster. Actually, I have to admit that this time he wasn't much of a klutz. Only a few little things happened. What was interesting is that Jackie decided to enter the science fair. And he wants to do a very interesting project. Have you ever seen those miniature erupting volcanoes? Jackie wants to build one. (Leave it to Jackie to choose the messiest possible project!) What have I gotten myself into?

Jessi

It was the evening of the science fair. I was so excited, you'd think *I'd* entered a project in it. (Well, in a way I had.) Anyway, the kids who were entering had to arrive at Stoneybrook Elementary by six-thirty in order to set up. The fair itself began at seven-thirty.

So at six-thirty, there were Stacey and Charlotte, Mal and Margo, Kristy and David Michael, Jackie and me, and a whole lot of kids and their parents or brothers or sisters or grandparents. Actually, Jackie and I had arrived at 6:20 to make sure we got our table staked out.

Now, at nearly seven o'clock, the all-purpose room was noisy and busy. All around Jackie and me were sighs of relief (when things went right) and groans (when things went wrong). Kids walked by carrying everything from huge pumpkins to complicated electrical things. I could hear the sounds of gears turning, tools tinkering, and video equipment. The all-purpose room was a pretty exciting place to be in.

"How do you feel, Jackie?" I asked him.

His volcano was loaded up and ready to explode. The "Welcome to the World of Volcanic Activity" sign was hung. His pointer was in his hand.

"Fine," he replied, but he sounded nervous. "Listen to this: Igneous rocks are born from fire, the molting—"

"Molten," I corrected him.

"The molten rock that lies several feet—"

"Miles."

"Okay. Several miles below the surface of our wonderful earth."

"Just *our earth*, Jackie. Don't overdo it."

Jackie nodded miserably.

Seven-thirty. The all-purpose room had really filled up. Teachers and parents and families and friends were pouring in.

"Look!" cried Jackie. "There are Mom and Dad and Archie and Shea!"

Boy, did Jackie seem relieved.

The Rodowskys made a beeline for The World of Volcanic Activity.

"Your project looks great, son," exclaimed Jackie's father.

AWESOME!

Would you believe more than 100 million Baby-sitters Club books have been sold!

WELCOME to the WORLD of Volcanic Activity

"Yeah, it really does," Shea managed to admit.

"You know what?" I said. "I think I'm going to look around at the other projects before the judging begins. Jackie, you stay here and answer questions—but don't set the volcano off, okay?"

Jackie laughed. "Okay." He was beginning to feel pleased with himself. Even Shea hadn't seen the volcano explode. Jackie couldn't wait for the big moment. He wanted to prove something to Shea who, as his big brother, was always several steps ahead of him.

I walked slowly around the room, looking at the displays and experiments. I saw a model of a human heart made from Play-Doh (I think). I saw a small-scale "dinosaur war." I saw an impressive project about the Ice Age. I saw Charlotte's plants with her charts and graphs. One plant was considerably more healthy-looking than the other two, which were sort of scraggly.

"Which plant is that?" I asked, pointing to the full, green one.

"Guess," she said.

"The one that listened to classical music."

"Wrong." Charlotte grinned. "It's the Duran Duran plant. I'm not sure why. Maybe they were just really *fresh* seeds."

I laughed, and continued my walk through the exhibits. When I got back to Jackie's display, I found his family preparing to take a look around, so I said I'd stay with Jackie.

The volcano attracted a lot of attention.

"Neat! What's that?" asked a curly-headed boy.

"A volcano," said Jackie proudly. "It can *erupt*. It makes ash and lava go everywhere. It's really messy."

"Can I see?" asked the boy.

Jackie's face fell. "Sorry. I can only make it explode once. I have to wait until the judges are here. You can see it then."

"Okay," said the boy, looking disappointed.

A few seconds later two girls walked by.

"A volcano!" exclaimed one. "Hey, I've always wondered. What *does* make a volcano?"

Jackie was prepared. "Igneous rocks are born from fire…" He said the entire speech without one mistake. I gave him the thumbs-up sign.

The girl frowned. "But *why*," she went on, "do igneous rocks do that? I mean, why does heat make a volcano erupt?"

HANDCRAFTED

It usually takes Ann Martin a month to write a Baby-sitters Club book. And she doesn't use a typewriter or a computer. She writes each book by hand!

Jackie was stumped. That wasn't part of his speech. And he couldn't demonstrate the volcano to the girls, either.

Just when I was beginning to feel bad, my own family showed up. Well, Mama and Daddy and Becca did. Squirt was at home with Aunt Cecilia. Becca had come because she wanted to see Charlotte's experiment, and my parents were there because of the volcano they'd been hearing about.

I began to feel better.

At eight o'clock, an announcement came over the PA system.

"Attention, please. May I have your attention? The judging will now begin. All participants in the science fair prepare to demonstrate and explain your projects to the judges. Visitors, please stand at the back of the room during the judging."

"That was our *princ*ipal," Jackie informed me.

(You'd have thought the President of the United States had just spoken.)

"Good luck, Jackie," I said. "I know you'll do fine. When it's time to make the volcano erupt, tell the judges you have to call me to light the match because you're not allowed to do that yourself."

Jackie swallowed and nodded. I joined my family at the back of the room.

The judging began.

Two women and a man walked solemnly from table to table. They looked each project over. They requested demonstrations. They asked questions.

WELCOME to the WORLD of VOLcanic Activity

Asked questions? Oh, no! Jackie couldn't talk about anything that wasn't in his speech. I hoped fervently that the judges would be so impressed with his demonstration that they wouldn't ask him any questions.

Tick, tick, tick. It was almost eight-thirty.

At last the judges reached The World of Volcanic Activity. I saw Jackie whisper something to one of the women. Then he saw me in the crowd and motioned for me to come forward. I did so, matches in hand.

"This," said Jackie as I reached his table, "is Jessi. She's my helper. She has to light the match for me."

(The judges smiled.)

I lit the match, told everyone to stand back, and tossed the match in the volcano. Jackie threw his hands in the air and cried, "The miracle of a volcano comes to life before our very eyes!"

PHOO! Lava was everywhere! It almost spattered the judges. Then it settled into a nice gooey flow down the sides of the volcano. The judges looked extremely impressed.

I stood to the side as Jackie made his speech, using the pointer.

The judges nodded and smiled. And then the questions began.

"How," asked the man, "is the crater of a volcano created?"

"Um," said Jackie. He looked at me, but I couldn't help him. "Um," he said again. "I don't know." At least he didn't admit that I'd practically done the project for him.

"Well … what happens to the lava when it has flowed out of the crater?" asked one of the women.

"It—it's very hot…" Jackie said lamely.

I looked at the ground. This was my fault. I felt terrible as I watched the judges make notations on their pads of paper. They walked on to the last project of the fair without even telling Jackie, "Good work," or "Nice going."

I went back to my parents and waited guiltily and nervously for the results of the fair to be announced.

"Jackie's project was great!" Dad said to me. "I've never seen such a thing. You really helped him."

A little too much, I thought.

Several minutes later, another announcement crackled over the loudspeaker. "The judges," said the principal, "have reached their decisions." (The judges were standing in the center of the room.) "They have chosen first-, second-, and third-place winners. When the winners are announced, will they please receive their

ribbons from the judges? Thank you." There was a pause. Then the principal continued. "Third prize goes to Charlotte Johanssen for her project entitled 'The Power of Music.'"

Applause broke out. Charlotte, looking shy but pleased, edged over to the judges, received her yellow ribbon, and scurried back to her table, where she proudly attached the ribbon to the sign she'd made for her project.

The next two winners were announced. They went to kids I didn't know. I sought out Kristy, Mal, and my other friends in the crowd. Except for Stacey, they looked as disappointed as I felt.

But nobody looked more disappointed than Jackie, even though an Honorable Mention ribbon was already being fastened to his desk. (Every kid except the three winners was given an Honorable Mention.) The Rodowskys and I crowded around The World of Volcanic Activity.

"Don't be too upset, honey," Mrs. Rodowsky told Jackie.

I had to speak up. "He has a right to be upset," I said.

Mr. and Mrs. Rodowsky turned to me. "Why?" they asked at the same time.

"Because—because I gave him so much help with his project that he really didn't do much of it himself."

"Yeah," said Jackie, giving me the evil eyeball.

"I'm really sorry," I went on. "I just wanted him to win. He's always saying he's no good at anything, or that he has bad luck. I wanted him to see that he *can* be a winner. I guess I went about it all wrong, though."

Mr. and Mrs. Rodowsky were really nice. They understood what had happened. I got the feeling that they might have done things like this for Jackie in the past. Mr. Rodowsky even admitted to building the glass and wood box for the volcano himself. (Well, with a *teeny* bit of help from Jackie.)

But Jackie, who's usually so easygoing and sunny, continued to scowl at me. "I just wanted to have fun," he said. "That was all. I just wanted to make a volcano erupt."

"Jackie, Jessi apologized to you," his father said gently.

"I know." Jackie finally managed a smile. But it quickly turned to a frown. "Oh, no," he muttered. "Here come John, Ian, and Danny. They're going to laugh at me. I just know it."

But the three boys who approached us looked excited.

"Jackie," said one, "your volcano was totally rad. Make it explode again!"

"Yeah," said another. "That was so cool."

Jackie explained why he couldn't "explode" the volcano again.

"Oh, well," said the boys. "It was still awesome."

They started to walk away. "See you in school on Monday!" one called over his shoulder.

Jackie grinned at me like the Cheshire Cat. "I don't believe it!" he cried.

Mr. and Mrs. Rodowsky were smiling, too. "You know," said Jackie's mom, "there'll be another science fair next year. Jessi, maybe you could try helping Jackie again."

"I don't think so," I said. "I better not."

"Good," replied Jackie. "Because if I'm going to lose, I want to do it all by myself!"

A CENTURY of Hits

They're in books, in movies, on TV, and on your computer screen. They're almost everywhere you look. Who are they? Your favorite characters!

1900   1910   1920

1902

Peter Rabbit

The Tale of Peter Rabbit hopped to fame as the best-selling children's book ever.

1924

The Boxcar Children

All aboard! The author longed to live in a caboose. She couldn't, but she created characters who did.

Batman

Batman didn't start out with his trademark cape and costume. At first, the artist drew him with stiff bat's wings and a red outfit!

1939

Madeline

There are actually two Madelines. One is the French school girl. The other is . . . the author's wife!

Lassie

A dog named Pal was the first Lassie. The latest Lassie is Pal's great-great-great-great-great-grandson.

1943

1950

Ramona

The world's most famous pest lives on Klickitat Street, a real street in Portland, Oregon. The author grew up just a few blocks away.

1930   1940   1950

1931

Babar

Babar began in France as a bedtime story. The well-dressed elephant now stars worldwide in books, on TV, and on cassette.

1950

Charlie Brown

The *Apollo 10* astronauts named their command ship *Charlie Brown*. Naturally, they called the lunar module . . . *Snoopy!*

1962

Clifford

Talk about big! This red dog isn't just a book and video. He's a giant balloon in New York's Thanksgiving Day Parade.

1963

Encyclopedia Brown

The boy detective speaks only English. But his adventures have been translated into 14 different languages!

1969

Kermit the Frog™

Kermit started out being a lizard! He was changed into a frog just before he made his bow on *Sesame Street*.

1960

1970

1963

Amelia Bedelia

Who but Amelia Bedelia would put sponges in sponge cake? The author, that's who! She tried out *all* of Amelia's recipes.

1971

Chapulin Colorado

The "red grasshopper" leaped over the border from Mexico. Now he struts his stuff on Spanish-language TV channels here.

Carmen Sandiego

Where is Carmen Sandiego? Millions of players track her across their computer screens. They chase her on TV, too!

1988

Iktomi

Iktomi is a trickster in the folklore of the Lakota people. He's so tricky that he goes by at least 10 different names!

1981

Julian

Where do stories come from? Author Ann Cameron got some of hers from the true adventures of her friend, Julian DeWetts.

1985

1980

1990

2000

1986

The Baby-sitters Club

Call these baby-sitters and what do you get? One of the country's most popular middle-grade series.

1986

Ms. Frizzle

The Friz drove the Magic School Bus right off the page and onto your television screen.

1996

The Animorphs

Why change? Ask the Animorphs. The five teens in this hit fantasy series try to save the world by morphing into any animal they choose.

Think About Reading

Answer the questions in the story map.

Beginning

1. Why does Jessi attend the science fair?

2. How does Jackie feel? Why?

Middle

3. What happens when the judges ask questions about Jackie's volcano?

4. How does Jackie feel after the prizes are announced? Why?

Ending

5. Why does Jessi tell Jackie that she's sorry?

6. What does Jackie say about next year's science fair?

Write a Diary Entry

Imagine you are Jessi. Write a diary entry for the Baby-sitters Club Notebook. Tell about what happened at the science fair. Describe how you felt. Tell what you will do differently next year.

Literature Circle

Did the story end the way you wanted it to? Think of a new ending for the story. Then talk about how the rest of the story would have to change to fit the new ending. Make a flow chart to show the new events and the new ending.

Author
Ann M. Martin

Ann M. Martin says that she writes her books for herself as well as for her readers. She has always loved books. When she was a child, she set up a library in her room for neighborhood children. She even charged a fine if someone returned a book late! Helping others is very important to Ann Martin. That's one reason why the girls in the Baby-sitters Club are always so active in their community.

More Books by Ann M. Martin

- *Abby and the Best Kid Ever*
- *Mary Anne to the Rescue*
- *Baby-sitters Summer Vacation*

How to
Create a New Episode

Write a story outline for a new episode in a series.

Hooray! A new book in your favorite mystery series just arrived in the bookstore. How does the author keep writing new episodes? The answer is simple. It takes imagination and knowing what kids like. You can also find hit series on television, at the movies, in comics, and in cartoons. No matter where you look, there is always a new episode to read or watch.

COMPUTER GAMES

MOVIES

COMICS

BOOKS

Look at a Series

Put on your thinking cap. It's time to come up with an idea for a new episode in your favorite series. First, choose a fiction series you like. It can be a book, cartoon, or a comic strip series that you read, or a TV, movie, or computer game series that you watch.

TOOLS

- paper and pencil
- markers or colored pencils

Then, take a close look at the series. Answer these questions.

- Who are the main characters?
- Where and when does the series take place?
- Is the series funny, serious, exciting, or scary?

Tips You can get ideas from:
- stories you have read.
- places you know.
- events in your life or someone else's life.

2 Think of a Story Idea

Create a brand new story for the series you have chosen. Imagine what might happen if:

- the characters go to a new place—a farm, the ocean, a city, outer space, or a park.

- a new character joins the series.

- the characters discover an unusual object, win a contest, or start a business.

Write down your ideas for a new episode. Choose the one you like best.

How Am I Doing?

Before you begin to write your story outline, stop and ask yourself these questions:

- Is the episode about characters in a series?

- Do I know what will happen in the episode?

Write a Story Outline

Now you have an idea for a new episode in your favorite series. Like all good stories, your episode should have a beginning, a middle, and an end. You can tell about the episode by writing a story outline. The outline doesn't have to be long. But it does need to give details about the story.

Here are some things you can include in your story outline:

- a list of the characters and a short description of each

- a couple of sentences telling where and when the episode takes place

- a short description of what happens in the episode

LASSIE:
My
Story

By

Julian's Camping Trip
Place: The Beach
Time: summer
Characters:
Julian
Huey, his
Glori

Julian's
Camping Trip

4 Present Your Story

Make an eye-catching cover for the story outline of your new episode. On it, write the series title, the episode's title, and your name.

Then, illustrate the cover with a scene from the story. Place your story outline in the classroom library. Read the story outlines written by your classmates. Did anyone write a new episode for the same series as you did? How are the episodes similar and different?

If You Are Using a Computer ...

Make your episode's cover look really great! Experiment with different kinds and sizes of type for the title and your name. If you use the Sign format, you can place a decorative border around the title page.

BATMAN'S BIG ADVENTURE

CONGRATULATIONS

Now you have become a real hit-series author. Can you spot which new books, TV shows, and movies will become hit series?

Joanna Cole and Bruce Degen
Author and Illustrator ▶

THEME
Finding information in stories and artifacts brings the past to life.

www.scholastic.com
Visit the kids' area of **www.scholastic.com** for the latest news about your favorite Scholastic books. You'll find sneak previews of new books, interviews with authors and illustrators, and lots of other great stuff!

UNIT 5

LITERACY PLACE

Archaeological Site

Finding information in stories and artifacts brings the past to life.

HOME PLACE

BY CRESCENT DRAGONWAGON

ILLUSTRATED BY JERRY PINKNEY

AWARD
WINNER

Every year,
these daffodils come up.
There is no house near them.
There is nobody to water them.
Unless someone happens to come this way,
like us, this Sunday afternoon, just walking,
there is not even anyone to see them.
But still they come up, these daffodils
in a row, a yellow splash
brighter than sunlight, or lamplight, or butter,
in the green and shadow of the woods.
Still they come up, these daffodils,
cups lifted to trumpet
the good news
of spring,

though maybe no one hears
except the wind
and the raccoons who rustle at night
and the deer who nibble delicately
at the new green growth
and the squirrels who jump
from branch to branch
of the old black walnut tree.

But once,
someone lived here.
How can you tell?
Look. A chimney, made of stone,
back there, half-standing yet, though honeysuckle's
grown around it—there must
have been a house here. Look.
Push aside these weeds—here's
a stone foundation, laid on earth.
The house once here was built on it.

And if there was a house, there was
a family.
Dig in the dirt, scratch deep, and what
do you find?
A round blue glass marble, a nail.
A horseshoe and a piece
of plate. A small yellow bottle. A china doll's arm.

Listen. Can you listen, back, far back?
No, not the wind, that's now. But listen,
back, and hear:
  a man's voice, scratchy-sweet, singing "Amazing Grace,"
  a rocking chair squeaking, creaking on a porch,
  the bubbling hot fat in a black skillet, the chicken frying,
  and "Tommy! Get in here this minute! If I have to call you
  one more time—!"
  and "Ah, me, it's hot," and "Reckon it'll storm?"
 "I don't know, I sure hope, we sure could use it,"
  and "Supper! Supper tiiiiime!"

If you look, you can almost see them:
the boy at dusk, scratching in the dirt with his stick, the
uneven swing hanging vacant
in the black walnut tree, listless in the heat;
the girl, upstairs, combing out her long, long hair, unpinning,
unbraiding, and combing, by an oval mirror;
downstairs, Papa washing dishes as Mama sweeps the floor
and Uncle Ferd, Mama's brother, coming in, whistling, back
from shutting up the chickens
for the night, wiping the sweat
from his forehead.
"Ah, Lord, it's hot, even late as it is,"
"Yes, it surely is."
Someone swats
at a mosquito.
Bedtime.

But in that far-back summer night,
the swing begins to sway
as the wind comes up
as the rain comes down
there's thunder there's lightning (that's just like now)
the dry dusty earth soaks up the water
the roots of the plants, like the daffodil bulbs
the mama planted, hidden under the earth, but alive
and growing, the roots
drink it up. A small green snake
coils happily in the wet woods,
and Tommy sleeps straight through the storm. Anne, the girl, who
wishes for a yellow hair ribbon, wakes and then returns to
sleep, like Uncle Ferd, sighing as he dreams
of walking down a long road with change in his pocket. But
the mother wakes, and wakes the father, her husband,
and they sit on the side of the bed,
and watch the rain together,
without saying a word, in the house where everyone else
still sleeps. Her head on Papa's shoulder,
her long hair falling down her back, she's wearing
a white nightgown
that makes her look
almost like a ghost when the lightning flashes.

And now, she *is* a ghost, and we
can only see her
if we try. We're not sure
if we're making her up, or if
we really can see her, imagining
the home place as it might have been, or was, before
the house burned down, or everyone moved away
and the woods moved in.

Her son and daughter, grown and gone, her brother
who went to Chicago, her husband, even
her grandchildren, even her house,
all gone, almost as gone as if
they had never laughed and eaten chicken and rocked,
played and fought and made up,
combed hair and washed dishes and swept,
sang and scratched at mosquito bites.
Almost as gone, but
not quite. Not quite.
They were here.
This was their home.

For each year, in a quiet green place,
where there's only a honeysuckle-vined chimney
to tell you there was ever a house
(if, that is, you happen to travel that way,
and wonder, like we did);
where there's only a marble, a nail, a horseshoe, a piece
of plate, a piece of doll,
a single rotted almost-gone piece of rope swaying
on a black walnut tree limb,
to tell you there was ever a family here;
only deer and raccoons and squirrels
instead of people
to tell you there were living creatures;
each year, still,
whether anyone sees, or not,
whether anyone listens, or not,
the daffodils come up,
to trumpet their good news
forever and forever.

141

OWL
MAGAZINE
ARTICLE

Meet

AWARD WINNER

The Missing Marble Case

Many years ago, in 1925, a boy stood on the porch of Gore Vale mansion (see left) with his friends. As he played with a marble in his pocket, it fell out, rolled across the porch, and over the edge into the dirt below. There it stayed until it was found by the team of dirt detectives—over 60 years later!

Gore Vale mansion, 1925

BOYS CLUB

the Dirt Detectives!

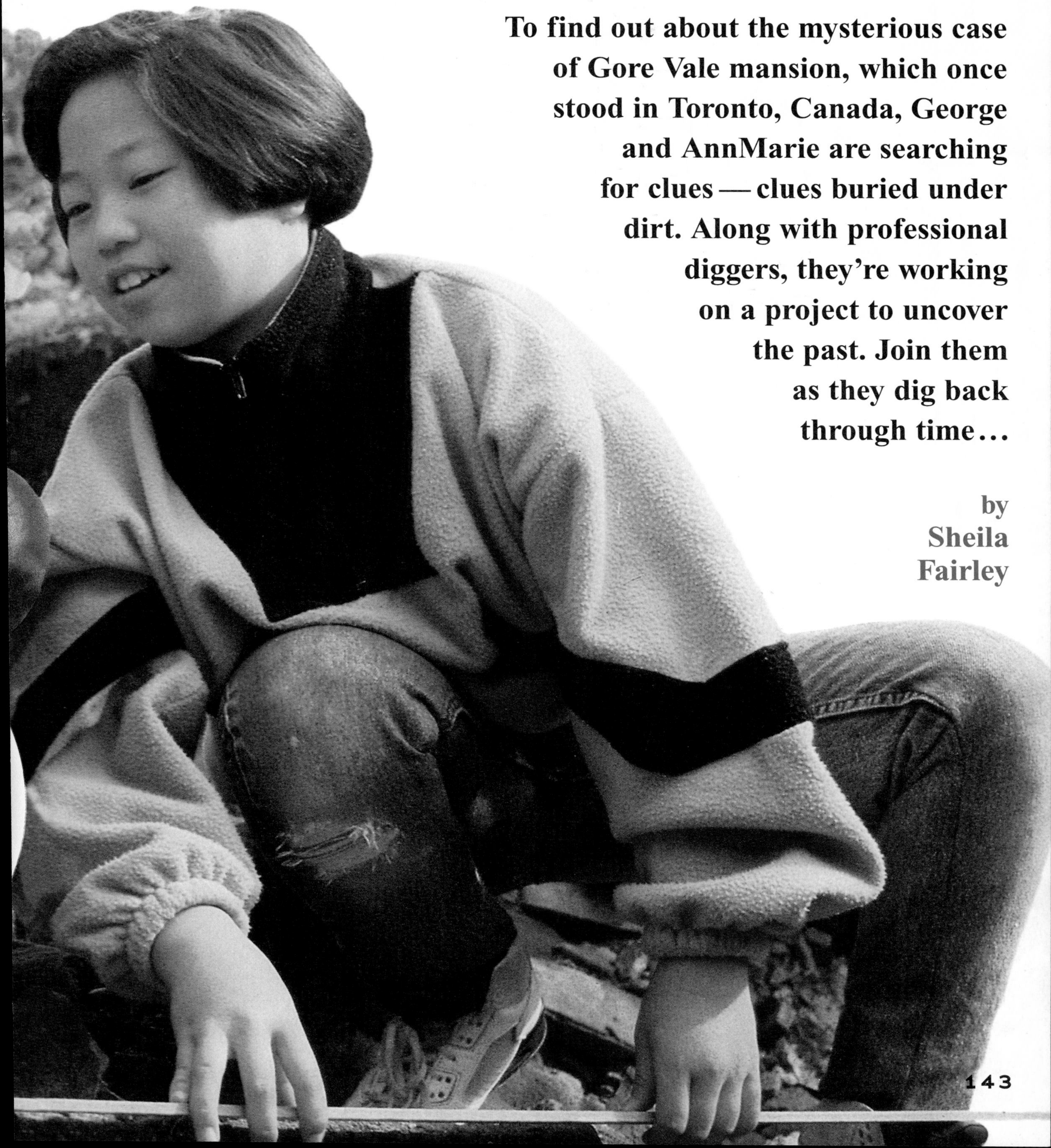

To find out about the mysterious case of Gore Vale mansion, which once stood in Toronto, Canada, George and AnnMarie are searching for clues — clues buried under dirt. Along with professional diggers, they're working on a project to uncover the past. Join them as they dig back through time…

by
Sheila
Fairley

OWL: How did you get interested in digging in the first place?

George: My mom told me about it and so did my uncle who's a teacher.

AnnMarie: I knew a bit about it before coming here with my class, but I had never been on a dig.

OWL: When you first came on the dig, did you have any idea of what you expected to find?

George: I didn't really think I would find anything, but I was lucky. The first day I found a nail, some brick chips and a piece of glass.

OWL: Now that you've worked on this project, has it changed the way you think about the past?

AnnMarie: Before, I thought it was boring, but now I see it's not. We have two hours for a dig but it goes by so fast, it feels like a few minutes!

Paintbrush for brushing away dirt

Trowel for digging

Meter stick for measuring things you find

Map to record details about where you're digging

Paper bag for storing things you find

Measuring tape for measuring larger things

Dustpan for collecting dirt

Whisk broom for cleaning the area you're in

The Story of Gore Vale

1820
Gore Vale mansion is built.

OWL: What's the most interesting thing that you've found while digging?

AnnMarie: I found part of an old china dish. You could only see part of the pattern and it was very colorful.

OWL: Was it different from the kind of dishes that we use today?

AnnMarie: Yes, the china felt like plastic.

OWL: Is there something about digging that you don't like?

George: You have to wait for a long time and you have to go slowly. I would like to be able to go a little faster.

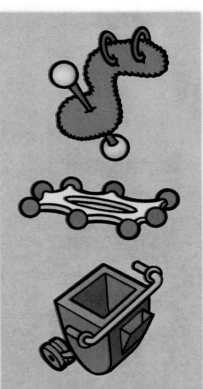

Imagine travelling to another planet and discovering these objects. What do you think they could be used for?

OWL: If you could leave something behind for future diggers to find, what would it be?

AnnMarie: Clothes . . . baggy jeans, and polo shirts.

George: I would probably write a letter or bury a time capsule. I'd write about the things we do.

OWL: What's the most important thing you'd like to share with OWL readers about digging?

George: Don't dig anywhere without checking because it may be against the law—and it could be dangerous!

AnnMarie: If you get a chance, try it—it's really fun. You have to wait, you have to be patient and you never know when something's going to turn up. But when it does, it's a surprise.

1925
Gore Vale is turned into a boy's club and then torn down.

1946
Family housing is built where Gore Vale once stood.

TODAY
Dirt detectives at work!

145

Think About Reading

Answer the questions in the story map.

SETTING

1. Where does the story take place?

CHARACTERS

2. Who is hiking in the woods?

3. Who once lived in the house?

BEGINNING

4. What does the girl find in the woods?

MIDDLE

5. What does the girl imagine that the family members are doing?

6. What might have happened to the house?

ENDING

7. Even though the house is gone, what still grows there every year?

Write a Friendly Letter

Imagine that you are the girl who discovers the ruined house. Write a letter to a friend about your finds. Describe what you saw. Include as many details as possible. Tell how you felt. Be sure to include a date, a greeting, and a closing in your letter.

Literature Circle

Talk about how the girl in *Home Place* is different from George and AnnMarie in "Dirt Detectives." Tell how she is like them. What does the girl find? What do George and AnnMarie find? How are their ways of finding artifacts different? Record your ideas on a Venn diagram.

Author
Crescent Dragonwagon
Illustrator
Jerry Pinkney

Author Crescent Dragonwagon was born Ellen Zolotow, but in the late 1960s she changed her name. She has written almost forty children's books since then. She says, "Good writing, for a reader of any age, comes from the heart."

Award-winning illustrator Jerry Pinkney chooses the books he works on carefully. He says, "I'm looking, first of all, for an exciting story to work on."

Another Book by
Crescent Dragonwagon
and Jerry Pinkney
• *Half a Moon and One Whole Star*

NONFICTION

WILD and WOOLLY
MAMMOTHS

by ALIKI

A wild and woolly beast once roamed
the cold northern part of the earth.
It had two great, curved tusks
and a long, hairy trunk.
Its big bones were covered with tough skin
and an undercoat of soft, woolly fur.
Over that, its long shaggy coat of hair
reached almost to the ground.
It was an ancient kind of elephant
called a woolly mammoth.

Woolly mammoths flourished thousands of years ago.
Long, long before then, when dinosaurs lived,
the earth was hot and swampy.
But temperatures changed.
Parts of the earth grew cold.

In some places in the north, the snow never melted.

It froze over and formed thick sheets of ice called glaciers.

This was the time of the Ice Age.

Many animals died out because of the cold.

Other animals did not die out.

They migrated to warmer places and survived.

Still others remained in the cold north.

Every year, vast herds roamed across the icy plains
of Europe, Asia, and North America.

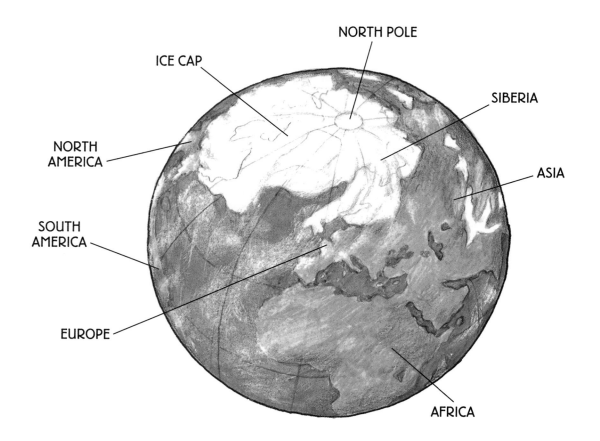

NORTH POLE

ICE CAP

SIBERIA

NORTH
AMERICA

ASIA

SOUTH
AMERICA

EUROPE

AFRICA

Only animals with heavy coats of hair, like the woolly mammoth, were able to survive the freezing cold.
Their warm covering protected them.

GIANT ELK
(Megaloceros species)

WOOLLY RHINOCEROS
(Coelodonta antiquitatis)

MUSK OX
(Ovibos species)

BISON
(Bison species)

IBEX
(Capra species)

WOOLLY MAMMOTH
(Mammuthus primigenius)

These animals were also protected from the cold by fat. The woolly mammoth had a hump of fat on its back and head, and a three-inch layer of fat on its body.

It happened long ago
that one of these woolly mammoths
fell into a deep crack in a glacier.
It broke some of its bones and died.
Snow and ice covered its body.
The cold preserved its flesh.

Thirty-nine thousand years passed.
Slowly the weather grew warm again.
The thick layers of ice began to melt.
The Ice Age had ended.

In 1900, the mammoth's body was discovered in Siberia.

Part of it was poking out of the melting ice.

Travelers noticed their dogs sniffing the thawing meat.

The travelers did not know it was a mammoth, but it was.

Scientists uncovered the frozen body.

Only the exposed part had thawed and rotted.

The buried part was perfectly fresh—preserved by the ice.

Dogs ate some of the meat, and liked it,

even though it was thousands of years old.

Later, it is said, scientists tasted the mammoth flesh too,

and lived to brag about it.

The mammoth's last meal was still in its stomach.

It too was preserved by the cold.

And what a meal!

A mammoth thirty pounds of plant food.

A Mammoth's Diet
pinecones · pine needles · lichen · moss · twigs · grasses · ferns · flowers

More recently, scientists made another amazing discovery
in the stomach of a mastodon, a relative of the mammoths.
In the digested remains, they found live bacteria—
still preserved after 11,000 years.
The bacteria are the oldest living organisms ever found.

MAMMUT
Mastodon
found in Newark, Ohio, in 1989

Scientists found more woolly mammoths frozen in ice.

They found other kinds of mammoths, too, and studied them.

Now they know a great deal about these prehistoric animals.

"Mammoth" means giant, and they were.

Mammoths were the largest land mammals of their time.

They lived in various parts of the world, in diverse climates.

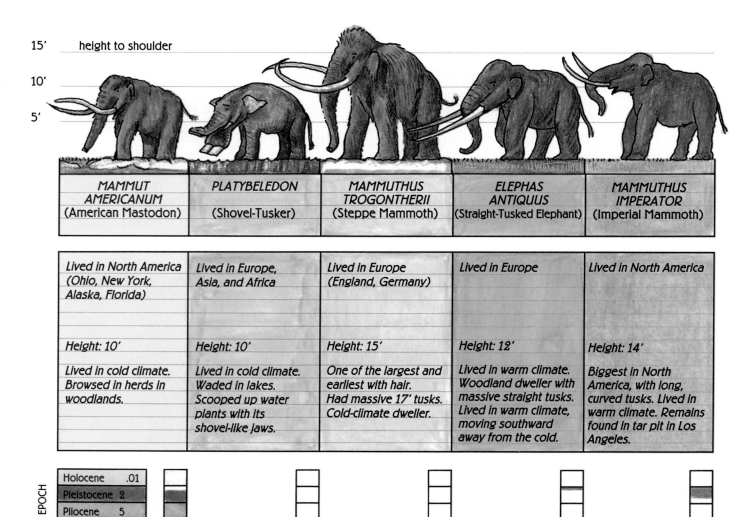

	MAMMUT AMERICANUM (American Mastodon)	PLATYBELEDON (Shovel-Tusker)	MAMMUTHUS TROGONTHERII (Steppe Mammoth)	ELEPHAS ANTIQUUS (Straight-Tusked Elephant)	MAMMUTHUS IMPERATOR (Imperial Mammoth)
Location	Lived in North America (Ohio, New York, Alaska, Florida)	Lived in Europe, Asia, and Africa	Lived in Europe (England, Germany)	Lived in Europe	Lived in North America
Height	Height: 10'	Height: 10'	Height: 15'	Height: 12'	Height: 14'
Description	Lived in cold climate. Browsed in herds in woodlands.	Lived in cold climate. Waded in lakes. Scooped up water plants with its shovel-like jaws.	One of the largest and earliest with hair. Had massive 17' tusks. Cold-climate dweller.	Lived in warm climate. Woodland dweller with massive straight tusks. Lived in warm climate, moving southward away from the cold.	Biggest in North America, with long, curved tusks. Lived in warm climate. Remains found in tar pit in Los Angeles.

EPOCH

Holocene	.01
Pleistocene	2
Pliocene	5
Miocene	25

MILLIONS OF YEARS AGO

Mammoths belonged to the Elephantidae family,
in an ancient group of Proboscidea—a group that includes
mammoths, mastodons, and modern elephants.
They are all animals with long trunks and tusks, hoofs,
and the flat teeth of plant eaters.
Today, only two species of elephants survive—those of Asia and Africa.
They are the last of the proboscideans, which first appeared
more than 50 million years ago.

15'   height to shoulder

10'

5'

ELEPHAS FALCONERI (Dwarf Mammoth)	MAMMUTHUS COLUMBI (Columbian Mammoth)	MAMMUTHUS PRIMIGENIUS (Woolly Mammoth)	ELEPHAS MAXIMUS (Modern Indian Elephant)	LOXODONTA AFRICANA (Modern African Elephant)
Lived on Mediterranean islands (Crete, Malta, Cypress, Sardinia)	Lived in southeastern North America (Carolinas, Georgia, Louisiana, Florida) and California	Lived in Europe, North America, Asia	Lives in Asia	Lives in Africa
Height: 3'	Height: 12'	Height: 9'	Height: 8-10'	Height: 13-14'
A dwarf island elephant. Lived in warm climate. Some island species survived for thousands of years after mainland species became extinct.	Had long, twisted tusks. Lived in warm climate in grasslands.	Shaggy, cold-climate tundra dweller. Hunted by early people. Not as big as some elephants, but powerful, and with a massive head.	Warm climate, feeds on leafy vegetation. Threatened by loss of habitat.	Lives in warm climate. Threatened by poachers, who kill it for its ivory tusks.

Mammoths traveled in peaceful herds.
In warmer seasons, they moved from grassy plains
to winding rivers, searching for food and water.
They shared their habitat with other plant eaters—
bison, horses, musk oxen, and caribou.
Sometimes they were attacked by smaller, fearless
carnivores—cats, wolves, or bears.
But there was one hunter even more dangerous
than the fierce saber-toothed cat, *Smilodon*.
That was the human hunter.

The mammoth hunters were cave dwellers.
They needed mammoths to live.
They hunted mammoths and other animals
with weapons they made of stone.
So their time is called the Stone Age.

Not long ago, remarkable wall paintings
were discovered in dark, damp caves.
They were made by Stone Age artists.
The paintings show the animals people hunted at that time—
mammoths, camels, bison, aurochs (ancient cattle), and horses.
Many of these animals are now extinct.
Artifacts, too, were found. They were carved in ivory,
bone, and stone, and tell about life long ago.

*Horse carved from
mammoth tusk
found in Germany*

*Bison and plants
carved in bone knife
found in France*

*Head carved in ivory
found in France*

More discoveries were made by archaeologists—
scientists who study ancient ruins.
They uncovered the remains of a whole Stone Age village.
They learned many things from this village and others like it.
They found out how mammoth hunters lived, and how
important the mammoth was to them.

In winter, clans lived in caves and in rock shelters,
protected from the cold.
In the spring, the snow began to melt.
The clans moved down to river valleys, where the
mammoths would come to graze.
Men, women, and children worked in groups.
They picked fresh grains, roots, grasses, herbs, and berries.
They collected bones of animals that the river washed down.
They used them to build elaborate shelters, covered
with mud and animal skins.
Then they prepared for the dangerous mammoth hunt.

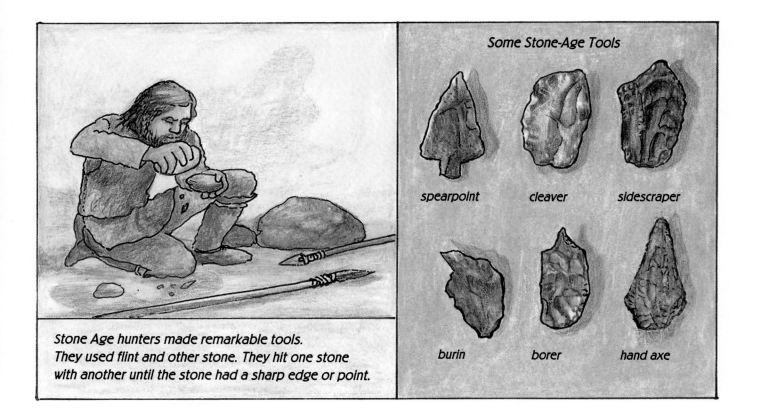

Some Stone-Age Tools

spearpoint   cleaver   sidescraper

burin   borer   hand axe

Stone Age hunters made remarkable tools.
They used flint and other stone. They hit one stone
with another until the stone had a sharp edge or point.

Toolmakers chipped knives, axes, and other tools
out of stone and mammoth bone.
They made razor-sharp spearpoints and attached
them to long, wooden spears.
With these, the hunters would kill the mammoths.
But first they had to find them and trap them.
Often they traveled far from their camps looking for them.

Sometimes the hunters set fires around the herds.
Then they forced the frightened beasts down steep cliffs.
Other hunters waited below to kill the mammoths with their spears.

Sometimes the mammoth hunters dug deep pits. They covered the pits with branches, bones, and earth.

When a mammoth walked over the pit, the cover collapsed, and the mammoth fell in.

It could not escape.
Hunters rolled heavy stones
down on the trapped mammoth
and killed it.

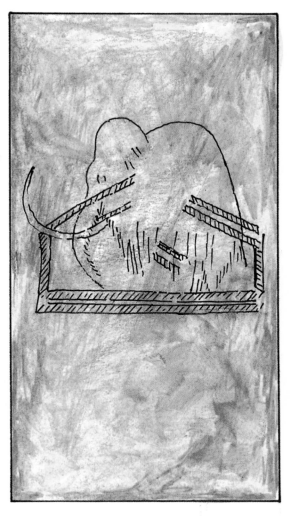

Stone Age wall painting
found in a cave in France.
It shows a mammoth
caught in a pit trap.
Many mammoths that
were discovered showed
that their bones
had been broken,
and they had been
butchered with knives.

Other animals were hunted for food and clothing too,

but a mammoth was a prized catch.

One was big enough to feed many people for a long time.

The group worked as a team to skin and butcher

the giant beast, and they saved nearly all its parts.

It was hard work.

They removed the brains and soft organs.

They cut and sliced the meat into pieces.

They removed the tusks, saved the fat and hide,

collected the bones.

They hauled it all back to their campsite.

Then they probably had a big celebration.

People used the skulls, tusks, and bones
for the foundations of their shelters.
It sometimes took the bones of 95 mammoths
to make one shelter.
They piled the bones around their camp, ready for use.

They used the mammoth's heavy hide as a door flap,
and cut it into strips for cords.
They twisted the long hair cording for mats,
and used the woolly fur for bedding.
They burned bones for fuel.
They boiled the nourishing fat into a rich brew,
and used the fat for food, drink, medicine,
curing hides, and many other purposes.

They made musical instruments out of the skull, bones, and tusks.
They used the stomach and intestines
as containers and cooking pots.
They carved the ivory tusks into jewelry, basins, utensils,
needles, buttons, ornaments, and sculptures.

They dried the fresh meat
to preserve it for winter.
They also stored and preserved
fresh meat in deep pits
they dug in the permafrost,
the permanently frozen ground
beneath the thawed, spongy soil.

Mammoth hide was too heavy to be used for clothing. Garments were made mostly of deer and bison skins and furs.

Season after season, herds of mammoths
continued to roam the tundras, steppes, and valleys
of the north.
Season after season, hungry cave dwellers
hunted them down.
This could be one reason why they died out.
No one is sure.

Today, elephants and many other animals
are also at risk of dying out.
People are concerned.
Many find ways to protect the animals,
to save them from extinction.

Mammoths were not so lucky.
Now we have only ancient remains
to tell us of their existence.
We can only imagine how it was when
wild and woolly mammoths roamed the earth.

Dr. Ruben Mendoza

Archaeologist

Archaeology is fun. Can you dig it?

Can a broken dish tell you a story? The answer is yes, if you are an archaeologist. Archaeologists are time detectives. They look for ancient artifacts—things that people made or used. Even an old dish can tell these scientists a lot about people who lived long ago.

PROFILE

Name: Dr. Ruben Mendoza

Born: French Camp, California

Job: assistant professor of archaeology at the University of Colorado

Hobbies: travel and photography

Most exciting find: arrowheads found near Denver, Colorado, that are about 11,000 years old

Where he would go if he were a time traveler: back in time 1,400 years to an ancient city in Mexico

177

QUESTIONS
for Dr. Ruben Mendoza

Here's how one time detective, Dr. Ruben Mendoza, finds clues to the past.

Q How did you become interested in archaeology?

A I went on a trip to Mexico when I was twelve. I became fascinated by the pyramids there. Being Mexican-American, I thought about the forgotten people who had built them. I even wondered if one of my ancestors had worked on them.

Q Weren't you recently on an archaeological trip in Mexico?

A Yes, I went with a group of archaeologists and students. We were on a dig. We use that word because we dig up things from the past.

Q What is the first thing you do on a dig?

A Before we do any digging, we lay a grid of string over the whole area. Then we make a paper map showing the same thing. That way, we can record on the map where each artifact is found.

Q **How do you know where to start digging?**

A We look for clues. We might start at a circle of stones that could be the remains of an old fireplace. Or we might dig into a mound—a small hill. This could be a spot where people left things behind.

Q **What do you learn from clues found on a dig?**

A Sometimes we find stone knives and bone needles. These show that ancient people knew how to make and use tools.

Q **Are all artifacts found underground?**

A No. Sometimes we find petroglyphs. They're drawings, usually found on a rock cliff or on the wall of a cave. They often picture animals that lived in the area.

Q **What do you do with artifacts you find on a dig?**

A Each artifact is given a number, then weighed and measured. Drawings and maps are photographed. We write all these facts on a card, along with the date, place, and name of the person who found it. Later, this information goes into a computer file so it's easy for others to study. The artifacts themselves end up in a museum.

Dr. Ruben Mendoza's `Tips`
for Young Archaeologists

1 If you find an artifact, record exactly where you found it.

2 Study the place where you discovered the artifact. Read about the people who once might have lived there.

3 Give the artifact to a museum. Take along the records you have kept.

179

THINK ABOUT READING

Write your answers.

1. Why did the woolly mammoths survive when the weather turned cold?

2. How do you know that the Stone Age people were not wasteful?

3. Think about the discoveries in the selection. Which one do you wish you had been present at? Why?

4. Why did Aliki include illustrations with captions in *Wild and Woolly Mammoths*?

5. Which parts of *Wild and Woolly Mammoths* might Dr. Ruben Mendoza find most interesting? Why?

WRITE A SCIENCE LOG ENTRY

Imagine that you are one of the scientists who dug up a frozen mammoth. Write an entry in your log about what you saw and what you did. Write the date of your entry. Include facts and details about what you found. Tell why the discovery is important.

LITERATURE CIRCLE

Aliki used many different sources to write *Wild and Woolly Mammoths*. What different kinds of information did she include? Where do you think she found the information? How do you think she knew what to draw? Make a chart showing the kinds of information she included in her book and where they might be found.

AUTHOR/ILLUSTRATOR
ALIKI

Author and illustrator Aliki has loved to draw since she was a little girl. In fact, her kindergarten teacher thought she would be an artist one day. Today Aliki does more than draw. She writes books about things that interest her. She says, "Writing and illustrating books is a way of satisfying my curiosity. I'm lucky that children are as curious about things as I am." Aliki has written more than 40 books since she began writing in 1961.

MORE BOOKS BY
ALIKI

- *Digging Up Dinosaurs*
- *How a Book Is Made*
- *My Visit to the Aquarium*

How to Create an Artifact Exhibit Card

artifact
described in
the card

How do you learn about the past? One way is to look at artifacts in a museum. You might discover a toy from ancient Egypt or an arrowhead made thousands of years ago. To learn more about each artifact, you can read the exhibit card that goes with it.

What is an exhibit card? An exhibit card gives information about an artifact—when it was made, who made it, what it was made of, and how it was used.

name of artifact

size

ARMOR OF GEORGE CLIFFORD, THIRD EARL OF CUMBERLAND

Blued steel decorated with gold designs

Made in Greenwich, England, sometime between 1580 and 1585

Height: $69\frac{1}{2}$ inches

The third earl of Cumberland wore this armor when he attended tournaments. At the tournaments, knights showed off their skills. This fancy armor was made for him at the royal armor shops in Greenwich. When the earl dressed in his armor, he had to put on fourteen different pieces. They were held together with leather straps. Each piece was made of strong plates of steel held together with metal pins. This made the armor flexible, so the earl could move easily.

This armor was purchased by the Muncie Fund in 1932.

materials used

where and when artifact was made

description— includes interesting details

information about how the museum acquired the artifact

1 Choose an Artifact

Think of all the different kinds of "artifacts" you use in a day, at home or at school. They might be for eating, traveling, doing schoolwork, playing sports, or getting ready for bed. They might be in-line skates, a fancy pencil, or a baseball cap. Choose an artifact that you would like to see in a museum.

TOOLS

- paper and pencil
- large index card
- an artifact

2 Collect Information

Gather as much information as you can about your artifact. What is it? How is it used? Where was it made? Where is it used? What is it made of? Who uses it? Is there anything unusual about it? Does it have any decorations? Keep notes on your discoveries.

Tips
- Look at the artifact carefully.
- Think of what you already know about it.
- Read labels and any writing on it.
- Read about it in a reference book.

3 Write Your Card

Use the information you've gathered to write your exhibit card.

- On the index card, write the artifact's name.
- Below the name, write a short paragraph about the artifact.
- Include interesting facts.

Place your artifact with its exhibit card.

4 Create an Exhibit

With your classmates, set up a museum exhibit called "Things We Use." Put artifacts that are similar together. For example, artifacts about school might go in one group. Artifacts about hobbies might go in another. Display each artifact with its exhibit card. Now tour your museum. Look at all the artifacts. What did you discover about the time you live in?

If You Are Using a Computer ...

Create your exhibit card using the Poster format. Browse through the collection of clip art for an artifact to show on your card. Choose an attractive border to make your card complete.

THINK

Imagine that you could travel a hundred years into the future. What artifacts from today do you think you might find?

Dr. Ruben Mendoza
Archaeologist ▶

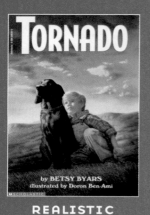

REALISTIC
FICTION

TORNADO

by BETSY BYARS
illustrated by Doron Ben-Ami

The Storm

"Twister!" Pete yelled. "Twister!"

I ran for the house.

"Twister!"

He pointed.

I looked over my shoulder. I could see it—a long, black funnel cloud in the west. It pointed from the dark sky right down to our farm.

Pete opened the doors to the storm cellar and beckoned with his straw hat.

"Twister!" he shouted again.

My two brothers ran from the barn. Pete helped my grandmother down the steps.

"Hurry up, boys," she called. Then she said to my mother, "Come on, Beth."

My mother was standing outside the door. She was worried about my daddy.

"Link! Link!" she called. My daddy had been named for a president. "Lincoln!"

"He's in the cornfield," Pete said. "He can't hear you, ma'am."

Still my mother hesitated. The cornfield seemed to be directly under the funnel.

"He'll be all right. He can get in a ditch. You come on now."

She ducked into the cellar, and Pete pulled the doors shut behind her.

The storm cellar was dim and cool. It smelled of potatoes and pickles. My mother kept sacks of root vegetables here along with boxes of eggs and jars of tomatoes.

My brothers and I sat on the dirt floor. My grandmother sat on a pickle barrel and my mother on an orange crate.

We sat for a moment, silent. We listened to the storm and worried about my father in the cornfield.

Something that sounded like gravel was thrown against the cellar doors.

"Hail," my mother said, and bowed her head.

Pete cleared his throat. "You know what this brings to mind?" he said.

We knew, and my brothers and I turned to him gratefully. We saw a flash of teeth as he smiled at us.

"It brings to mind a dog I had one time."

"Tornado," my brothers and I said together.

"How'd you know his name?" he teased. "Yes, I did call my dog Tornado."

Pete settled his straw hat on his head and began. "I remember it was an August day, a whole lot like this one."

The Doghouse

At breakfast that morning, I remember my mother looked up from the stove, took a breath, and said, "I smell a storm."

I shivered a little, because my mother's nose was always right.

My daddy said, "Well, you kids better stay close to the house."

The morning went by, slow and scary. We did stay close to the house. Folks didn't call our part of the country *Tornado Alley* for nothing.

Along about lunch, it hit. Only there was no warning like we had today. No funnel cloud, no nothing. One minute we were eating beans and biscuits at the table. Next there was a roar—worse than a train—worse than a hundred trains. And then there came a terrible tearing sound, like the world was being ripped apart. I can still hear it in my mind.

I looked up, and I saw sky. The ceiling was clean gone. There was the sky! The tornado had torn the roof off the kitchen and left the food on the table and us in our seats.

My daddy was the first to be able to speak. He said, "Well, I'm surprised to find myself alive."

That was how we all felt. We looked at our arms
and legs to make sure they were still hooked on us.
Then my father pushed back his chair and said,
"Let's go see the damage."

Outside, the yard was not our yard anymore.
The tree with the tire swing was laid flat. The tops
of all the pine trees had been snapped off. A
doghouse I had never seen before was beside the
well. A piece of bicycle was here, the hood of a car
there. I stepped over somebody's clothesline that
still had some clothes on it.

The roof of the kitchen lay at the edge of the
garden. It was folded shut like a book. We walked
over there.

"It was about time for a new roof," my daddy
said. He always tried to find the good in
something.

I was just walking around, looking at other
people's things, when I heard a rattling noise.

I kept listening and looking, and finally
I realized the sound was coming from that
doghouse. I went over to it.

The doghouse was trembling. You could see it.
It was trembling. It was shaking. It was doing
everything but having a fit.

I looked inside, and there was a big black dog. He was panting so hard, I could feel his breath. He was shaking so hard, the doghouse was in danger of losing its boards.

"Daddy, there's a dog in here!"

My daddy came over.

"Look, Daddy. It's a big black dog."

My daddy leaned down and took a look.

"Well, you can come on out now," he told the dog. "The storm's over, and you're among friends."

The dog just kept shaking.

"Maybe I can pull him out," I said.

"Don't you put your hand in there," my mother said.

"Yes, leave him be, Pete."

All that day, all that night, all the next day that dog shook. I brought him water, but he wouldn't drink. I brought him food, but he wouldn't eat.

Then that night my mother leaned out the kitchen door and yelled, "Supper!" as she usually did. The dog heard her and stuck his head out of the doghouse. He must have been familiar with the word.

He came out, stood there, looked around for a moment, and then gave one final shake, as if he were shaking off the past. Then he came over and joined us at the back door.

I said, "Daddy, can we keep him? Please?"

"If we don't find the owner."

"Can we call him Tornado?"

"Until we find the owner."

"We'll have to ask around," my mother reminded me.

"I know."

My daddy bent down. "Let's see what kind of manners you got, Tornado. Shake!"

My daddy put out his hand. Tornado put out his paw. They shook like two men striking a bargain.

Then we all went in to supper.

A Card Trick

"Speaking of Tornado," Pete went on, raising his voice over the sound of the wind, "reminds me of something funny that happened one time."

He waited, as if for encouragement.

"Is it about the three of hearts?" I asked quickly.

"Well, you already know the story. You don't want to hear it again."

"I do! I do! This is my favorite story in the world."

"Well, maybe it won't hurt to tell it one more time."

Back in those days, my little brother, Sammy, and I played cards in the evening. We liked to play a game called "War," but we were not supposed to play it because that's what it turned into, and my mother was tired of listening to us fight.

Anyway, there we were in the kitchen, at the table, when Tornado came up and poked my leg. He did that when he wanted my attention, to remind me his dish was empty or something.

But there was food in his dish, and there was water in his bowl. "You got everything you need. Stop poking me."

I went back to the card game, but Tornado poked me again.

"It's too dark to go for a walk," I said.

He poked me again.

I said to Sammy, "If I didn't know better, I'd think Tornado wants to play cards!"

Sammy said, "Then play cards with him. I'm tired of this stupid game."

Because he was losing, Sammy threw down his cards and left the room.

I looked down at Tornado. "You want to play cards?" I asked.

Tornado looked at me. His ears came forward as if he were interested. I held the cards so he could see them. His ears came forward some more. I shuffled the cards. Now his ears were almost over his eyes.

"You want to play cards? Cards?"

I held out the deck. He waited. I fanned out the deck. He waited. I could see he was ready, willing, and able. He had that look he got when I had a ball and he was waiting for me to throw it.

Then I had an idea. I put one card out farther than the rest. "Pick a card, Tornado," I said. "Pick any card you want."

Tornado took one step forward. He stretched out his neck. He took the card. *He took the card!* I remember it to this day. It was the three of hearts. The dog was standing there with the three of hearts in his mouth!

Tornado stood there.

I sat there.

We waited.

The trouble was I didn't know what we were waiting for. I had a dog with the three of hearts in his mouth, a dog who could do a card trick, but I didn't know what the trick was.

"Put it back," I said, offering him the deck.

He didn't move. I tried to take the card from him and put it back myself, but he would not let go.

My daddy came in the kitchen for a glass of buttermilk. I said, "Daddy, Tornado knows a card trick!"

"Does he?"

"At least I think he does. Well, he knows half of a card trick."

"Half a card trick's better than none."

"See, I held out the cards like this, and he took one, but now he won't let it go."

"Tornado, drop it!" my daddy commanded.

Tornado dropped the card and wagged his tail.

"Good dog," my daddy said.

"Daddy, do you want to see the card trick? I think I can do it now."

"If it doesn't take too long. I want to hear the news."

I put the card back in the deck. It didn't want to go because it was wet now and there were teeth marks in it.

"Pick a card, Tornado, any card," I said.

Tornado picked a card. I crossed my fingers for luck. "Tornado, if that card is the three of hearts, drop it!"

Tornado waited.

"Drop it!" my daddy ordered.

Tornado dropped the three of hearts.

"Good dog," I said. I felt really proud. I had a dog who could do a card trick, even though my daddy had to help.

"Is that it?" my daddy said.

"Yes, sir. You can get back to the news."

"The news can wait. Let's try that trick again."

Carey's Turtle

"Telling that story always puts me in mind of the turtle."

"Turtle? You never told us about a turtle."

"Didn't I? Surely I told you about the turtle."

"No, you didn't, did he?"

"No," said my brother.

I said, "Was it your turtle?" to get him started. It worked.

Pete smiled.

As I recall it, the turtle belonged to a girl named Carey, and it was about the size of a silver dollar.

My sister, Emma Lou, was looking after the turtle, and I mean she was particular about it—gave it fresh water every day whether the turtle wanted it or not, and wouldn't let any of us so much as near it.

One nice sunny day Emma Lou changed the water as usual and put the bowl out on the porch so the turtle could get some sun.

An hour went by. When Emma Lou went out again, the turtle was gone. You never heard such carrying on.

"Who took Carey's turtle? Mama, somebody stole Carey's turtle!"

I expect you could have heard her all over the county.

My brother and I swore up and down we hadn't done it, but Emma Lou didn't believe us.

"Mama, make them tell me what they did with Carey's turtle. I know they stole Carey's turtle."

My mother had come out to referee, and was giving my brother and me a little talking-to about playing jokes on people, when I looked over and saw Tornado.

Tornado was sitting by the steps, and he had a look on his face like something was wrong.

I went over to him, and I noticed that his mouth wasn't closed all the way. I pulled up his lip and saw a turtle foot.

I closed the lip back up quick as I could, because I didn't know whether the turtle was alive or dead, but my brother had already seen it too and said, "The turtle's in Tornado's mouth. I saw its foot." He was glad to be innocent for once.

I knew right away what had happened. Tornado had come around the house, seen the nice bowl of water, leaned down for a drink, and ended up with a mouthful of turtle.

Emma Lou came over and held out her hand. "Tornado, give me Carey's turtle. And that turtle better be all right or you'll be sorry."

Tornado just sat there, looking more troubled than ever.

"Tornado, I mean it. Give me that turtle!"
Tornado didn't move.

"Tornado, if you don't give me that turtle right this minute— "

I didn't let her finish. I said in my father's voice, "Drop it!"

Tornado opened his mouth, and the turtle dropped into Emma Lou's hand. That turtle was good as new.

As soon as he dropped the turtle, Tornado went wild. He started running around the yard and around the barn and around the house. Sitting there for an hour with a turtle in his mouth and not knowing what to do with it must have been the worst thing that could happen to a dog. The only thing to do was run it off.

Well, it was catching. I started running along with him. Tornado would run around the tree one way and I'd run the other, and when we would almost bump into each other, it would make us run some more.

I don't know how long we kept it up, but finally we did bump into each other and just fell down on the ground.

"Good dog," I said when I got my breath back.

"Good dog?" Emma Lou said from the porch. "For lapping up Carey's turtle?"

"For keeping it safe," I reminded her.

"Oh, all right," she admitted. "Good dog."

from *Always Wondering*

Wind

by Aileen Fisher

The wind has lots of noises:

it sniffs,

it puffs,

it whines,

it rumbles like an ocean

through junipers and pines,

it whispers in the windows,

it howls,

it sings,

it hums—

it tells you VERY PLAINLY

every time it comes.

Gust of wind at Ejiri, in the province of Suruga. From the series The Thirty-Six Views of Fuji Hokusai, Metropolitan Museum of Art

In a gust of wind the white dew
by Bunya No Asayasu

In a gust of wind the white dew
On the Autumn grass
Scatters like a broken necklace.

Shira tsuyu ni
Kaze no fukishiku
Aki no no wa
Tsuranuki tomenu
Tama zo chirikeru

THINK ABOUT READING

Write your answers.

1. Why do Pete and the others hurry into the cellar?

2. Why do you think Pete tells stories while the family is in the cellar?

3. Imagine you were with Pete when he found the dog. What would you do? How would you feel?

4. How does the author help you imagine what it's like to be in the storm?

5. Which parts of Aileen Fisher's poem describe the sound of the wind in *Tornado?*

WRITE A CHARACTER SKETCH

Tornado was quite a dog. You learned a lot about him from Pete's stories. Now write a description of him. First, brainstorm a list of words that tell what Tornado looked like and how he acted. Think about what made him special. Then use your list to write about him. Try to make your readers feel as if they have really met Tornado.

LITERATURE CIRCLE

Everybody loves a good dog story. Talk about dog stories you have read, seen on TV, or watched at the movies. How was the dog in each story like Tornado? How was the dog different? Which stories were your favorites? Why?

AUTHOR
BETSY BYARS

Betsy Byars thinks of her books as scrapbooks of her life. She says, "When I see something quirky or real or interesting, I put it in a book." One of her favorite things is to give a character one of her own memories. Ms. Byars loves animals and has two pets—a dog and a cat, so it's not surprising that *Tornado* is about a big lovable dog. For fun, Betsy Byars reads, solves word puzzles, and flies airplanes all over the United States. She is always creating new memories to put in her books.

MORE BOOKS BY
BETSY BYARS

- *Beans on the Roof*
- *The Golly Sisters Go West*
- *The Dark Stairs: A Herculeah Jones Mystery*

from

Pueblo Storyteller

BY **DIANE HOYT-GOLDSMITH**
PHOTOGRAPHS BY **LAWRENCE MIGDALE**

My name is April. I live with my grandparents in the Cochiti (KOH-chi-tee) Pueblo near Santa Fe, New Mexico. Pueblo (PWEB-loh) is a Spanish word that means "village" or "town." Our pueblo is very old. The Cochiti people have lived on these lands for many hundreds of years.

For me there is a special time at the end of every day. After the work is finished and I am ready to go to bed, my grandmother and grandfather tell me stories from the past. Sometimes they tell about the legends of the pueblo people. Other times they tell about things that happened in their own lives.

My grandmother likes to tell about when she was a girl. She lived in a Tewa (*TAY-wah*) pueblo to the north called San Juan. She remembers autumn, a time when her whole family worked together to harvest and husk the corn crop. The corn came in many colors—red and orange, yellow and white, blue and purple, and even the deepest black.

Her family would sit in the shade of a ramada (*rah-MAH-dah*) built of cedar branches. Sheltered from the hot sun, the workers would remove the husks from a mountain of colorful corn. All the time they were working, they would laugh at jokes, sing songs, and share stories.

My grandmother tells me there were always lots of children around—her brothers and sisters, their cousins and friends—and they always had fun. My grandfather tells how the boys would use their slingshots to hurl stones at the crows who came too close to the corncobs that were drying in the sun.

As I listen to their stories, I can almost hear the sound of laughter as the children play at their games. I can smell the bread baking as the women prepare to feed their families. I can see the mounds of corn, colored like the rainbow, drying in the sun.

When I was very young, my grandparents told me a legend about how our ancestors found the place where we are living today, our pueblo along the Rio Grande River. They call it "How the People Came to Earth," and it is still one of my favorite tales.

How the People Came to Earth

◀◀◀◀◀◆▶▶▶▶

A PUEBLO LEGEND

Long, long ago, our people wandered from place to place across the universe. Their leader was Long Sash, the star that we call Orion. He was the great warrior of the skies. Long Sash told his people that he had heard of a land far away, a place where they could make a home.

Because the people were weary of wandering, they decided to follow Long Sash on the dangerous journey across the sky to search for a new home. They traveled on the Endless Trail, the river of countless stars that we call the Milky Way.

The way was hard for our people. Long Sash taught them to hunt for food, and to make clothing from the skins of animals and the feathers of birds. Even so, they were often hungry and cold, and many died along the way. Long Sash led them farther than any people had ever gone before.

After a time, the people came to a vast darkness, and they were afraid. But Long Sash, the great warrior, believed they were heading the right way, and led them on. Suddenly, they heard the faint sound of scratching. Then, as they watched, a tiny speck of light appeared in the distance. As they got nearer, the light grew larger and larger. Then they saw that it was a small hole leading to another world.

When they looked through the opening, they saw a little mole digging away in the earth. Long Sash thanked the mole for helping them to find their way out of the darkness. But the mole only replied, "Come in to our world. And when you see the sign of my footprints again, you will know you have found your true home." The people saw a cord hanging down from the hole and they all climbed up and went through into the new world.

Once through the opening, Long Sash saw Old Spider Woman busily weaving her web. He asked permission to pass through her house. Old Spider Woman replied, "You may come through my house. But when you next see the sign of my spiderweb, you will have found your true home."

The people did not understand what Old Spider Woman meant, but they thanked her and continued on their journey.

Long Sash and his followers traveled to many places on the earth. They found lands of ice and snow, lands where the sun burned and the air was dry, and beautiful lands with tall trees and plenty of game for hunting. In all of these places, they searched for signs of the mole and Old Spider Woman, but found nothing.

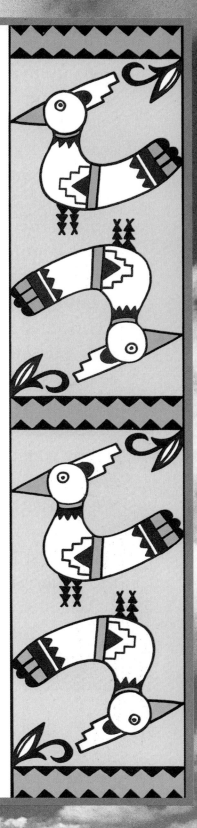

Some of the people stayed behind in the lands they discovered, but Long Sash and most of the tribe kept going. They kept searching for their true home.

Finally they came to a new land where the seasons were wet and dry, hot and cold, with good soil and bad. They found, here and there, small tracks that looked like a mole's. They followed the tracks and found a strange-looking creature, with ugly, wrinkled skin. The slow-moving animal carried a rounded shell on its back.

Long Sash was very happy when he saw the creature. "Look!" he said. "He carries his home with him, as we have done these many years. He travels slowly, just like us. On his shell are the markings of the spiderweb and his tracks look just like the mole's."

When our people saw the turtle, they knew they had found the homeland they had traveled the universe to discover. And we still live on those same lands today.

My grandparents are storytellers who have brought the past alive for me through their memories, through their language, through their art, and even through the food we eat. I am thankful that they have given me this rich history. From them I have learned to bake bread in an ancient way, to work with the earth's gift of clay, and to dance to the music of the Cochiti drums.

I am a pueblo child and I love to listen to my grandparents tell stories. From their example, I learn to take what I need from the earth to live, but also how to leave something behind for future generations. Every day I am learning to live in harmony with the world. And every day, I am collecting memories of my life to share one day with my own children and grandchildren.

CLUES
to the **PAST**
A to Z

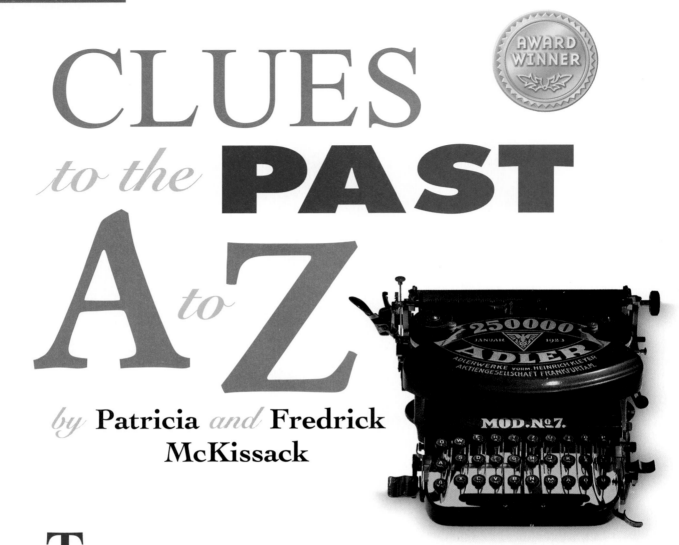

AWARD
WINNER

250000
JANUAR 1923
ADLER
ADLERWERKE VORM. HEINRICH KLEYER
AKTIENGESELLSCHAFT FRANKFURT AM.

MOD. No 7.

by **Patricia** *and* **Fredrick McKissack**

This is a book of artifacts. An artifact is an object from the past that can tell us something about the people who made and used it.

Follow the alphabet from A to Z to learn about 26 artifacts and their stories.

Happy exploring!

Arrowhead

Long ago, people used bows and arrows to hunt and wage war. They usually made arrowheads from materials such as shells, rocks, and bones found near their homes. Native Americans west of the Rocky Mountains probably shaped these arrowheads. The rocks they're made from are plentiful there.

Basket

Baskets were among the first objects people learned to make. They were beautiful as well as useful. These sea grass baskets were woven by African Americans. Their slave ancestors brought the art of basket making from Africa. They passed the skill down to their children and grand-children.

Coin

Coins often give us information about the past. This one-dollar coin was issued between 1979 and 1981 by the United States government. It honors Susan B. Anthony. During the 19th century, she worked for an end to slavery and for the right of women to vote.

Doll

We know that children have played with dolls for the last 3,000 years. This doll was found in an ancient Egyptian tomb. It gives us an idea of how Egyptian children dressed and wore their hair long ago.

Eyeglasses

This painting of Benjamin Franklin tells us an interesting story about eyeglasses. The famous inventor is wearing bifocals, which are special glasses that he designed in 1784.

Fabric

Long ago in Scotland, all the great families wore clothing made from specially designed fabric called tartan. You could tell which family a person belonged to by the tartan he or she wore. Today, Scots still wear their family tartan. But tartan plaids have also become popular with people all over the world.

Game

Yes, children played jacks and marbles over 3,000 years ago. Knucklebones was the ancient Greek form of jacks. And Roman children played with colored glass and pottery marbles.

Hat

In the American West, the cowboy's hat was more than a fashion craze. Cowboys used their hats to water their horses, and also as fans, umbrellas, drinking cups, and even as pillows.

the last drop from his STETSON

Ice skates

Ice skates like these were popular with Americans in the 1860s. The ankle strap was a new addition at that time. It helped people keep their balance.

Journal

Many travelers keep journals. Journals help us see a place as the traveler saw it. Meriwether Lewis and William Clark explored the land northwest of the Mississippi River between 1804 and 1806. Each of them kept a journal.

Kite

The Chinese were the first to make and fly kites. Their kites help us learn about Chinese culture and traditions. The Chinese flew kites to

celebrate births, marriages, holidays, and festivals. The butterfly kite is one of the oldest and most popular designs.

Lamp

In the 1800s, before electric lights were invented, many people used gas lamps to light their homes. Gas lamps were also used to light the streets at night.

Map

Long ago, people from the Marshall Islands made very accurate maps from grass reeds and sea shells. They used these maps to travel from island to island in the huge Pacific Ocean. Each cowrie shell marks the location of an island. The reed sticks show the direction of the waves between the islands.

Newspaper

Old newspapers are a great source of information about the past. *The New York Times* began publishing in 1851. It has kept a running diary of the day-to-day activities of ordinary and extraordinary people since the first day it went to press. What were the headlines on the day *you* were born?

Olla

For hundreds of years, Native Americans of the Southwest made clay jars called *ollas* (OH-yuz) to carry water to their homes. Ollas are still being made. Today they are sometimes used as water jars. But more often, they are collected as beautiful works of art.

Portrait

1861▶

1865▶

Every American president has been painted or photographed. Abraham Lincoln's portraits are among the most well known. These two photographs show how much he changed from the time he took office in 1861 until his death in 1865.

Quilt

This bride's quilt, from the 1850s, shows scenes from the bride's life. It tells the personal story of her courtship, engagement, and even her hopes and dreams for the future. When quilts are passed down from one generation to another, so are their stories.

Rug

The desert nomads of Persia were among the earliest known rug makers. They used their beautiful rugs in their daily lives. Persian carpets became very popular in Europe in the 1400s. Europeans used the one-of-a-kind rugs as wall hangings or table covers. They rarely used them on the floor!

Sundial

How did people tell time before there were clocks or watches? They often used sundials—sometimes portable ones like this one! The position of the sun's shadow on the dial showed the time. What happened when it was cloudy? People made a good guess.

Toy

Teddy bears are one of the best-loved toys in the world. They were named after President Theodore "Teddy" Roosevelt. In 1902, toymaker Morris Michtom saw a cartoon showing the President unwilling to shoot a bear cub. He made the toy teddy bear to honor the President.

Umbrella

The umbrella is an item we use to keep dry in the rain. But for the Asante people of West Africa, the umbrella was—and still is—a symbol of the king's power. There were hundreds of royal umbrellas. Each one had a special meaning. For example, when a king sat under an umbrella topped with a hen and baby chicks, it meant he was a judge settling arguments.

Vacuum cleaner

This is not an early fire engine! It's the original vacuum cleaner, invented in England in 1901. Men in uniform pulled it down city streets and offered to vacuum people's rugs. The machine remained on the street, and the hose was put through a window.

Weathervane and Whirligig

For many centuries people have wanted to know, "Which way is the wind blowing and how fast?" Long before there were TV weather forecasters, people put weathervanes and whirligigs on poles, rooftops, fences, and mailboxes to keep track of wind direction and speed. Today these objects are often used as decorations.

X-chair

The X-chair is one of the oldest kinds of folding furniture. The ancient Egyptians and Romans were the first to use X-chairs. They were easy for soldiers and hunters to carry. Later, European furniture makers called the X-chair a "scissor chair." Can you see why?

Yarn painting

The Huichol people of Mexico are known for their colorful yarn paintings. Each picture shows things that are important to the Huichol way of life—the sun, corn, sheep. For hundreds of years, these beautiful designs were painted or carved on rocks. Then the Huichol began to make their pictures with yarn.

Zither

Zithers were first made in China thousands of years ago. Different designs spread all over the world. During the 1700s, zithers like this one were brought to America by European immigrants. The zither is one of the instruments that gives Appalachian music its twangy sound.

Think About Reading

Write your answers.

1. What does April enjoy doing at the end of the day?

2. How can you tell that April's grandparents are proud of the Cochiti people?

3. Imagine that you lived in the San Juan pueblo when April's grandmother was a girl. What activities do you think you would have enjoyed most?

4. Why do you think the author of *Pueblo Storyteller* included a legend as part of the selection?

5. April's grandparents tell stories and use words to keep the past alive. Which artifacts in "Clues to the Past A to Z" also use words to tell about the past?

Write a Description

You have just visited April at the Cochiti Pueblo. Write a description of her. Tell what she looks like and how she dresses. Tell what she does for fun. Be sure to include colorful details in your description.

Literature Circle

Think of April's life in the Cochiti Pueblo. What kinds of stories might she tell her children and grandchildren? What artifacts do you think she might save to show them?

Author and Photographer
Diane Hoyt-Goldsmith and Lawrence Migdale

Diane Hoyt-Goldsmith often writes nonfiction books about children from different cultures. Her favorite part of writing books is getting to know the children and families who appear in her books. Many of them become "friends for life." Her books always include photographs by Lawrence Migdale.

More Books by Hoyt-Goldsmith and Migdale

- *Buffalo Days*
- *Potlatch: A Tsimshian Celebration*
- *Apache Rodeo*

How to Discover Picture Clues

How can we learn about people who lived 50, 100, or even 500 years ago? One way is to look for picture clues in old paintings or photographs.

What are picture clues? Picture clues are the details you see in paintings and photographs. These special clues show what life was like long ago—how people dressed, how they traveled, what they ate, and even what they did for fun.

Clothing was different from that worn by people today.

Horses were used for transportation.

The one-room schoolhouse was made of logs.

There were no other buildings nearby.

The children were different ages.

In Colorado during the late 1800s, children rode horses to school every day. Students in grades 1 through 8 all studied together in a one-room log cabin—and one teacher taught them all.

The caption tells about the photo.

1 Find a Picture

In your library, find an old picture with lots of details. It can be a photograph, a drawing, or a painting. Look in books and magazines. If you need help, ask your librarian. Or ask your family to find an old picture at home.

TOOLS

- old painting or photograph

- notebook

- pencil

- magnifying glass (optional)

2 Look for Clues

Look carefully at your picture. Take notes on what you see. These questions may help you.

- When was the picture taken?
- What place does it show?
- Who are the people in the picture?
- What are they wearing?
- What are they doing?

Do you notice anything else— toys, food, furniture, kinds of transportation?

3 Organize Your Notes

Scientists like Dr. Ruben Mendoza organize their notes. It helps them write about what they have found. You can use a chart to organize your notes about the old picture you looked at.

Place Colorado Time Late 1800's		
Things People Used	How People Traveled	What People Wore
Candles	horse back wagon	long dresses high button shoes big hats

Tip A chart can help you put similar details together.

4 Write a Caption

Now you can tell the world about the picture you chose. Look at your notes and chart. Decide which details are most important. Then write an informational caption that tells what is happening in the picture. Share the picture and caption with your classmates. Tell them what you discovered about the past.

If You Are Using a Computer...

Use your Newsletter format on the computer to make your organizing chart. Create columns and headings to help order your notes. If you like, you may also write the caption for your picture using a special font.

THINK

Archaeologists look at pictures for clues about how people once lived. What would a photograph of your classroom tell about school today?

Dr. Ruben Mendoza
Archaeologist ▶

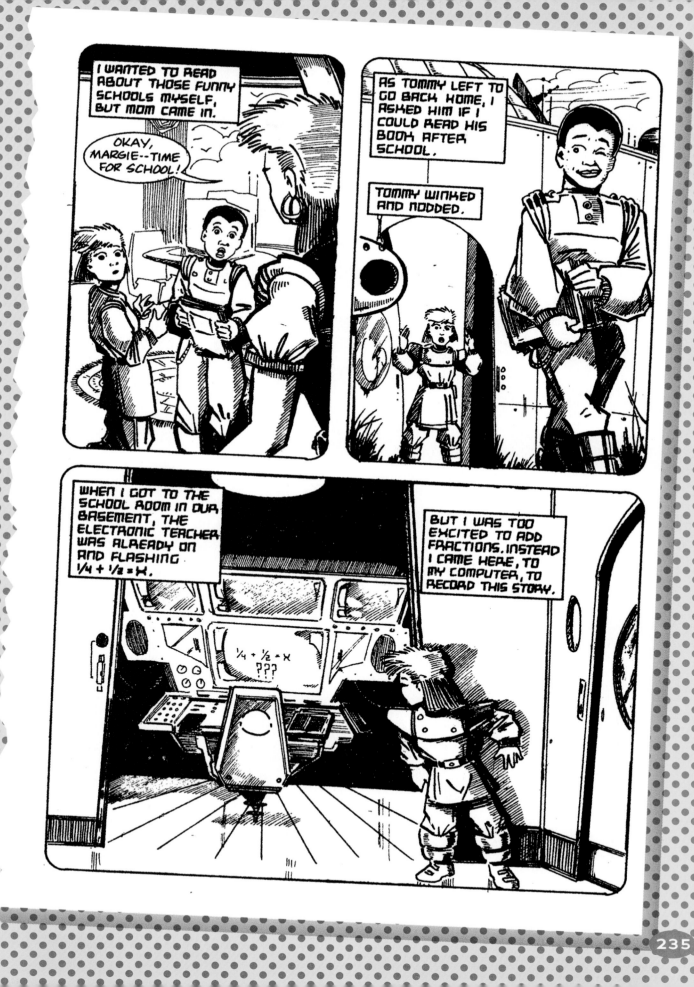

Into the Millennium

Scholastic News asked third graders around the country what they think the future will be like. Here is what some of them said.

There will be no school. We will learn from computers and robots at home.

**Megan Brock
The Dalles, Oregon**

Robots might do jobs that are dangerous for people and jobs like washing dishes. They could also become our friends.

**Casey Allison
Baraboo, Wisconsin**

Houses will have inflatable floats under them for any water emergency such as a flood or a hurricane.

**Cedric Mims
Cedar Hill, Texas**

Cars will be solar-powered. In the night they will be battery operated.

**Jamie Sanderson
Slaterville Springs,
New York**

We will visit other planets. We will make friends with people on other planets. Astronauts will have to learn lots of languages to communicate with others.

**Harry Gomez
Fairfax, Virginia**

Looking Ahead

Here is how some children responded to a poll.

		Yes	No
1.	Will kids go to school all year long?	32	68
2.	Will you need a computer to do your job?	62	38
3.	Will there be a cure for cancer?	88	12
4.	Will cats still be the most popular pet?	22	78

THINK ABOUT READING

Answer the questions in the story map.

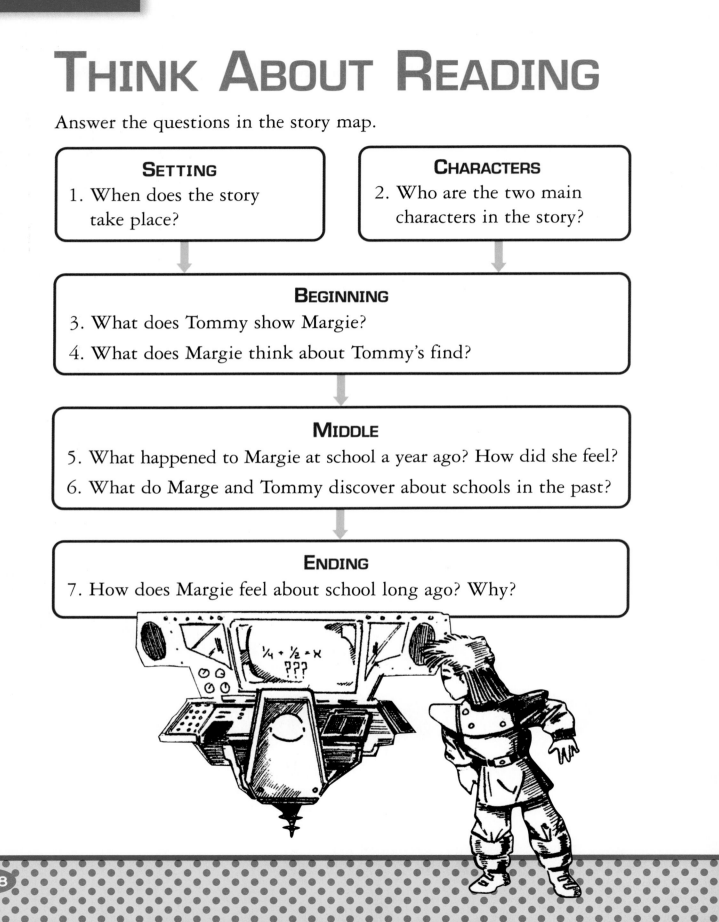

SETTING

1. When does the story take place?

CHARACTERS

2. Who are the two main characters in the story?

BEGINNING

3. What does Tommy show Margie?

4. What does Margie think about Tommy's find?

MIDDLE

5. What happened to Margie at school a year ago? How did she feel?

6. What do Marge and Tommy discover about schools in the past?

ENDING

7. How does Margie feel about school long ago? Why?

WRITE a DIARY ENTRY

In "The Fun They Had," Margie kept an electronic diary. Imagine you are Margie. Write another entry for her diary. In the entry, tell about an event in Margie's life. It might be about her favorite hobby or a trip she takes with her family. Make sure you include clues about life in 2155.

LITERATURE CIRCLE

How do you think life will change in the future? Talk about the predictions in "The Fun They Had" and "Into the Millennium." Which ones do you think will come true? Which ones will make life better? Take your own poll about the future and record the results on a chart.

AUTHOR
ISAAC ASIMOV

Isaac Asimov published his first story when he was a teenager. That was over fifty years ago. Asimov went on to write almost 500 science and science fiction books—more than any other author. He loved to explain difficult science topics and make up stories about the future. His hard work paid off. Today, he is still one of science fiction's best-known writers.

MORE BOOKS ABOUT THE FUTURE

- *The Best New Thing* by Isaac Asimov
- *My Robot Buddy* by Alfred Slote
- *2095 (The Time Warp Trio)* by John Scieszka

How to

Make a Time Capsule

Create a time capsule that tells kids in the future about life today.

Think about this. In the future, people will study us to learn what our lives were like. Someday your neighborhood may be an archaeological site! And someone may even find a time capsule buried there. A time capsule is a container that is filled with objects and information about a certain time and place. It gets stored away to be discovered sometime in the future.

1 Gather Artifacts

What can you put into a time capsule? You can put in anything that tells about your life as a third grader. It might be an empty box from your favorite cereal, a photograph of a popular sports star, a class picture, a magazine ad for a movie you like, or a list of this week's spelling words. You might even write a diary about a day at school.

Things to Put in a Time Capsule

- menus
- jokes
- photographs
- newspapers, magazines, or catalogs
- picture postcards
- recipes for favorite foods
- tapes of favorite songs

TOOLS

- paper and pencil
- index cards
- large waterproof container made of plastic or metal
- artifacts to place into your time capsule
- clear plastic bags
- paper folder

Gather as many artifacts as you can. Now put all your artifacts into one place. Look at them closely. Decide which ones best tell about life today. These will go into your time capsule. Make a list of the artifacts you want to use.

Tips
- Place paper artifacts into clear plastic bags.
- Don't choose foods, plants, or liquids.
- Make sure objects will fit into the time capsule.

2 Label the Artifacts

You can give kids of the future more information about each artifact, too.

- Make a label for each artifact. On an index card, write the name of the artifact, what it is, and why it is important to you.

- Then tape or tie the label to the artifact.

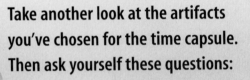

How Am I Doing?

Take another look at the artifacts you've chosen for the time capsule. Then ask yourself these questions:

- Is each artifact clearly labeled?

- Are the artifacts different from one another?

- Do all the artifacts together give a clear picture of life today?

Time Capsule

Artifact: Skates
In-line skating is a popular sport with many kids.

243

Greet the Future

Think of what you want to say to the kids who will open your time capsule. Write a short letter to them. Tell them about yourself. Describe what life is like today— what you like about it and what you would change.

Share your hopes for the future, too. Make a copy of your letter. Put it into a folder with your artifact list. Now you have a record of all the things you placed in your time capsule.

MILT THOMPSON Cardinals

2

4 Put the Capsule Together

Share your artifacts with the class, and tell why you chose each one. Then put your time capsule together. Carefully place your artifacts and the letter to the future inside the container you've chosen—a large plastic jar or a metal box with a tight-fitting lid. Close it up. If you like, decorate the outside of the time capsule.

When do you want your time capsule opened? In 10, 20, or even 50 years? Decide on a date in the future.

Find a place to store your time capsule. It might be in the principal's office or in your school library or in your schoolroom. Sometime in the future, another group of third graders will open it and discover what was important to you.

If You Are Using a Computer ...

Create a Journal entry on the computer about a typical day in your classroom. Then print it out to include in your time capsule. You also can write your letter to the future on the computer. Include clip art that tells about your life today.

These artifacts were collected by:

Date: *Place:*

Do not open until:

CONGRATULATIONS

Now you've become a real time detective. You can find clues to the past all around you. Keep looking for them!

Dr. Ruben Mendoza
Archaeologist ▶

Community Quilt

THEME
In a community, some things continue and some things change.

UNIT 6

Welcome to

LITERACY PLACE

Community Garden

In a community, some
things continue and
some things change.

THE Gardener

by Sarah Stewart
pictures by David Small

August 27, 1935

Dear Uncle Jim,

Grandma told us after supper that you want me to come to the city and live with you until things get better. Did she tell you that Papa has been out of work for a long time, and no one asks Mama to make dresses anymore?

We all cried, even Papa. But then Mama made us laugh with her stories about your chasing her up trees when you were both little. Did you really do that?

I'm small, but strong, and I'll help you all I can. However, Grandma said to finish my schoolwork before doing anything else.

Your niece,
Lydia Grace Finch

251

September 3, 1935

Dear Uncle Jim,

I'm mailing this from the train station. I forgot to tell you in the last letter *three important things* that I'm too shy to say to your face:

1. I know a lot about gardening, but nothing about baking.

2. I'm anxious to learn to bake, but is there any place to plant seeds?

3. I like to be called "Lydia Grace"— just like Grandma.

> Your niece,
> Lydia Grace Finch

On the train
September 4, 1935
Dear Mama,
   I feel so pretty in your dress that you made over for me. I hope you don't miss it too much.

Dear Papa,
   I haven't forgotten what you said about recognizing Uncle Jim: "Just look for Mama's face with a big nose and a mustache!" I promise not to tell him. (Does he have a sense of humor?)

And, dearest Grandma,
   Thank you for the seeds. The train is rocking me to sleep, and every time I doze off, I dream of gardens.
                    Love to all,
                    Lydia Grace

September 5, 1935
Dear Mama, Papa, and Grandma,
    I'm so excited!!!
    There are window boxes here! They
look as if they've been waiting for me,
so now we'll both wait for spring.
    And, Grandma, the sun shines down
on the corner where I'll live and work.
                Love to all,
                Lydia Grace
P.S. Uncle Jim doesn't smile.

December 25, 1935
Dear Mama, Papa, and Grandma,

I adore the seed catalogues you sent for Christmas. And, Grandma, thank you for all the bulbs. I hope you received my drawings.

I wrote a long poem for Uncle Jim. He didn't smile, but I think he liked it. He read it aloud, then put it in his shirt pocket and patted it.

> Love to all,
> Lydia Grace

February 12, 1936

Dearest Grandma,

 Thank you again for those bulbs you sent at Christmas. You should see them now!

 I really like Ed and Emma Beech, Uncle Jim's friends who work here. When I first arrived, Emma told me she'd show me how to knead bread if I would teach her the Latin names of all the flowers I know. Now, just half a year later, I'm kneading bread and she's speaking Latin!

 More good news: We have a store cat named Otis who at this very moment is sleeping at the foot of *my* bed.

Love to all,
Lydia Grace

P.S. Uncle Jim isn't smiling yet, but I'm hoping for a smile soon.

March 5, 1936
Dear Mama, Papa, and Grandma,
    I've discovered a secret place. You can't imagine how wonderful it is. No one else knows about it but Otis.
    I have great plans.
    Thank you for all the letters. I'll try to write more, but I'm really busy planting all your seeds in cracked teacups and bent cake pans! And, Grandma, you should smell the good dirt I'm bringing home from the vacant lot down the street.
                        Love to all,
                        Lydia Grace

April 27, 1936
Dearest Grandma,

All the seeds and roots are sprouting.
I can hear you saying, "April showers
bring May flowers."

Emma and I are sprucing up the
bakery and I'm playing a great trick on
Uncle Jim. He sees me reading my mail,
planting seeds in the window boxes,
going to school, doing my homework,
sweeping the floor. But he never sees me
working in my secret place.

Love to all,
Lydia Grace

P.S. I'm planning on a big smile from
Uncle Jim in the near future.

May 27, 1936
Dear Mama, Papa, and Grandma,
    You should have heard Emma laugh today when I opened your letter and dirt fell out onto the sidewalk! Thank you for all the baby plants. They survived the trip in the big envelope.
    More about Emma: She's helping me with the secret place. Hurrah!
                    Love to all,
                    Lydia Grace
P.S. I saw Uncle Jim almost smile today. The store was full (well, *almost* full) of customers.

June 27, 1936
Dear Grandma,

Flowers are blooming all over the place. I'm also growing radishes, onions, and three kinds of lettuce in the window boxes.

Some neighbors have brought containers for me to fill with flowers, and a few customers even gave me plants from their gardens this spring! They don't call me "Lydia Grace" anymore. They call me "the gardener."

Love to all,
Lydia Grace

P.S. I'm sure Uncle Jim will smile soon. I'm almost ready to show him the secret place.

July 4, 1936
Dearest Mama, Papa, and Grandma,

I am bursting with happiness! The entire city seems so beautiful, especially this morning.

The secret place is ready for Uncle Jim. At noon, the store will close for the holiday, and then we'll bring him up to the roof.

I've tried to remember everything you ever taught me about beauty.

Love to all,
Lydia Grace

P.S. I can already imagine Uncle Jim's smile.

July 11, 1936

Dear Mama, Papa, and Grandma,

My heart is pounding so hard I'm sure the customers can hear it downstairs!

At lunch today, Uncle Jim put the "Closed" sign on the door and told Ed and Emma and me to go upstairs and wait. He appeared with the most amazing cake I've ever seen—covered in flowers!

I truly believe that cake equals one thousand smiles.

And then he took your letter out of his pocket with the news of Papa's job!

I'M COMING HOME!

Love to all, and see you soon,
Lydia Grace

P.S. Grandma, I've given all of my plants to Emma. I can't wait to help you in your garden again. We gardeners never retire.

from *Cracked Corn and Snow Ice Cream*
by **Nancy Willard**
illustrations by **Jane Dyer**

JUNE ❧ the sixth month

flower Rose

FARMER'S CALENDAR

BIRTHSTONE
pearl
FOR HEALTH

HARVEST SCHEDULE	May	June	July	Aug.	Sept.	Oct.	Nov.
Apples							
Blueberries							
Melons							
Cherries							
Grapes							
Peaches							
Pears							
Plums							
Raspberries							
Strawberries							
Asparagus							
Beans							
Beets							
Broccoli & Cabbage							
Carrots							
Cauliflower							
Celery							
Corn							
Cucumbers							
Lettuce							
Onions							
Peas							
Peppers & Eggplant							
Potatoes							
Pumpkins							
Radishes							
Rhubarb							
Spinach							
Squash							
Tomatoes							

Plant late crops: squash, fall cabbages, rutabagas, and corn. Plant pumpkins at the edge of your cornfields to discourage raccoons: they dislike getting tangled in the vines.

Start your kitchen garden. Remember to make successive plantings of sweet corn, beans, peas, tomatoes, lettuce, and beets.

HOW TO KEEP MOLES OUT OF YOUR GARDEN:
Sink empty bottles into the ground around molehills, leaving a couple of inches of the necks showing above the soil. The wind blowing over the bottles will make a hollow sound, to the great annoyance of the moles.

Beans do well when planted in a mixture of soil and hair.

Pumpkins, cucumbers, and pole beans do not like to be planted near potatoes.

Spray your cucumber vines with sugar water. This will attract bees, and the vines will set more cucumbers.

 IN 1902 A FRENCH NATURALIST CLAIMED THAT IF ALL THE BIRDS SHOULD DISAPPEAR, HUMANS COULD NOT SURVIVE BEYOND NINE YEARS. SLUGS AND INSECTS WOULD DEVOUR ORCHARDS AND CROPS.

279

MENTOR

Lorka Muñoz

Community Garden Director

Learn why community gardens are here to stay.

Grow With Us
Community Garden

·KIDS' PLOTS AVAILABLE·

A GROW WITH YOUR NEIGHBOR'S GARDEN
of the Wegerzyn Horticultural Center
with the Support of the
City of Dayton's
Department of Planning

Take an empty city lot filled with rusty cans, plastic bottles, and weeds. Add a group of hard-working people, some flower and vegetable seeds, and a few trees. What do you have? "A community garden," says Lorka Muñoz with a big smile.

PROFILE

Name: Lorka Muñoz

Job: community garden director

Born: New York City

What *lorka* **means:** "Flower" in Russian. With a different spelling, it is also the last name of a famous Spanish poet.

Hobby: fixing up old houses

Most unusual garden you have seen: A kids' garden in Denver, Colorado. The kids used junk to make scarecrows

Community projects you did as a kid: planting trees

ALL ABOUT
Lorka Muñoz

Here's what Lorka Muñoz has to say about starting a community garden.

Lorka Muñoz works for an organization in Dayton, Ohio, called Grow With Your Neighbors (GWYN). She helps people all over the city turn empty lots into neighborhood green spots.

"A community garden usually starts with one or two people who have found a place for a garden," says Muñoz. "The first thing I do is meet with them and describe how GWYN can help. Then they start organizing other people in their neighborhood."

Lorka Muñoz has found that all kinds of people join Dayton's community gardens—young children, teenagers, parents, and grandparents. They all have one thing in common. They want to make their neighborhoods better places to live.

Getting a gardening group together and finding an empty lot are the first steps in creating a community garden. Then the fun begins. "The people at GWYN and the gardeners design the garden," says Muñoz.

Each garden has two parts. One is a community space—an area that everyone can use. Muñoz

helps the gardeners choose trees and ground covers to plant there. The rest of the garden is divided into small plots where each gardener can plant flowers and vegetables.

Before the planting can begin, the gardeners work together to clean up the lot. They haul away trash, dig up rocks, pull weeds, and prepare the soil. What a job! Then Muñoz helps them get the seeds, plants, and garden tools they need.

By the middle of the summer, the gardeners pick bouquets of flowers and harvest armloads of tasty vegetables. And they share their crops, too. "Some people grow more food than they can eat, so they give away the extra," says Muñoz.

Lorka Muñoz believes that community gardens help neighborhoods in many

ways. "People grow their own fresh food," she says. "Neighbors meet each other and begin to work together. And best of all, the neighborhood looks better."

Lorka Muñoz's
Tips for Improving Your Community

 Decide exactly what you want to improve.

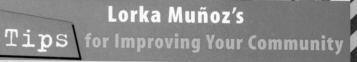 Share your idea with other interested people.

 Ask for help. Parents or other adults may be willing to lend a hand.

 Get started. Make a plan, and then carry it out.

Think About Reading

Write your answers.

1. Why does Lydia Grace go to the city to stay with Uncle Jim?

2. Who taught Lydia Grace about gardening? How do you know?

3. If you met Lydia Grace, what do you think you would like best about her?

4. Why do you think the author chose to tell Lydia Grace's story through letters?

5. Why would Lydia Grace and Lorka Muñoz make a great team?

Write a Name Poem

Lydia Grace is a colorful character. Write a name poem about her. First write the letters in her name down the side of a sheet of paper. Then write a sentence or phrase that begins with each of the letters. For the letter *L*, you might write, "Loves plants." Before you begin, brainstorm words and phrases that describe Lydia Grace. You can use a dictionary to help you find words for each letter.

Loves plants
Y
D
I
A

Literature Circle

In *The Gardener*, the award-winning illustrations give you information that isn't told in the story. Talk about the details you learn from the art. What are the characters like? What things change in the story? What are your favorite details?

Author
Sarah Stewart
Illustrator
David Small

David Small and Sarah Stewart team up to create picture books. Gardens are important to both of them. David Small happily remembers wandering through his grandmother's garden as a boy. It was one of the things that inspired him to become an artist. Like Lydia Grace in *The Gardener*, Stewart loves plants and flowers. In fact, she has five different gardens to keep her busy when she isn't writing.

More Books by
Sarah Stewart
and David Small

- *The Library*
- *The Money Tree*

Illustrated with *arpilleras* sewn by the Club de Madres Virgen del Carmen of Lima, Peru

IS CARNAVAL

BY ARTHUR DORROS

"Wake up, sleepyhead," my mother is calling. But I'm already awake. I'm thinking about Carnaval. This year I will play the *quena*, a flute, with my father in the band. "The quena is the voice of the band—the singer of the band," says Papa. Papa plays with the band every year at Carnaval. People in costumes will parade and dance to the music for three whole days and nights.

Carnaval is in the big village down the valley, and it's only three days away!

"We have a lot of work to do before then," Papa says. We work all year, almost every day, but not during Carnaval!

We get up each day before it is light outside, there is so much to do. Mama takes my little sister, Teresa, to the river to get water. Today Mama washes clothes, too. Papa and I look for firewood to use for cooking. Sometimes we walk a long way to find wood—there are hardly any trees in the high Andes Mountains of South America, where we live.

Today I bring my quena along, so I can practice special songs for Carnaval. A lot of the songs have a good beat that makes you want to dance. *Tunk tunk, tunk tunk.* Papa's ax chopping a log sounds like the beat of the *bombo*, the drum he will play with the band.

Back home Teresa drops kernels of corn into an empty pot. Mama will boil the corn for our meal. *Pling pling, pling pling pling.* The kernels make sounds like the strings of Uncle Pablo's *charango.* He will play in the band with us too, at Carnaval.

After our meal, we get a field ready for planting. I lead the oxen, to make sure they plow straight. Mama follows us and picks stones out of the loose earth. After Carnaval, my friend Paco and his family will help us plant potatoes. Sometimes Paco's family helps us in our field, and other times we help them in theirs. One of the songs I'm practicing for Carnaval is about working in the fields with friends.

After we plow, I take the hungry llamas high into the mountains to find grass. The best grass is by the crumbling walls of buildings made hundreds of years ago when the Incas ruled these mountains. No one knows how the giant stones were cut to fit together so well. Sometimes we use the old stones to build walls and houses and even terraces for the fields.

I sit on a wall and play my quena. I play a song called *"Mis Llamitas,"* "My Little Llamas," and the llamas leap and dance around. I imagine they are dancing to my music.

The wind whistling across the stones sounds like the windy notes of a *zampoña*, a panpipe. I will play my quena and Paco will play his zampoña when we meet at Carnaval. That's one of the things I like about Carnaval—we get together with friends from our mountain and from all around the valley.

One day is gone. Now we have only today and tomorrow before tomorrow night—when Carnaval begins. I can hardly wait. This morning Papa shears wool from an alpaca. An alpaca is like a llama, but with softer wool. I carry the wool to Mama, so she can spin it into yarn. "You don't have to run," laughs Mama. "Carnaval will come as soon as it can."

Mama's fingers twirl the wool round and round. She can spin yarn while she's walking, or selling vegetables, or doing almost anything. When she has enough yarn, she'll color it with different dyes. Grandma will weave it into cloth of many colors. Then Mama will cut and sew the cloth to make us clothes. Maybe she'll make me a new jacket.

In the afternoon, we dig potatoes out of the damp earth in a field we planted months ago. The digging usually makes me tired, but today I keep working as fast as I can to help harvest all the potatoes. Tomorrow we'll take them down into the valley to sell at the market. And after the market is cleared away, Carnaval will begin!

We gather red potatoes; yellow, black, and brown potatoes; even purple potatoes. In the Andes, we have hundreds of different kinds of potatoes.

We drop our potatoes into burlap bags, *plonk, plonk, plonk*. The llamas help carry the heavy bags to Antonio's truck. Antonio came from the village today, and he will sleep tonight in his truck.

Finally. Today we take the potatoes to market—then tonight is Carnaval!

I wait and wait to hear the truck start. The motor coughs and groans, *errr errr errr*. But at last Antonio gets it started. Mama, Papa, Teresa, and I—and the potatoes—bounce along in the back of the old truck, which rattles and shakes down the mountain. It stops like a bus to pick up people carrying onions, beans, carrots, turnips, peas, and peppers; llama wool; clothes; and food they have made for Carnaval.

"Hey," I hear someone say, "don't let that chicken eat our corn. We're taking it to market."

The truck bounces over a big bump. I reach down to make sure my quena is not broken. I want people to hear my quena sing when I play at Carnaval.

"Watch out flying over those bumps, Antonio," someone shouts. "Will this old truck fly us to the village?"

"Don't worry," Antonio shouts back. "This old truck and I know how to get there."

People hug when they climb into the truck. We don't see these friends very often. We all stand and look out along the way. People throw water balloons and water from buckets to try to splash us. They're excited about Carnaval.

At the market, I help unload the heavy bags of potatoes, and then I walk around. I love to see the brightly colored piles of vegetables. People trade wool that still smells like llamas or sheep. And the nutty smell of toasted fava beans and corn makes my mouth water.

But today I can't wait until Mama sells all of our potatoes and the market is cleared away. Then people will come out in their costumes. At first it will be hard to see who each person is—many of the people will be wearing masks. I'll find the band. Papa's bombo will start booming, Paco's zampoña will be whistling, and Uncle Pablo's charango plinging. People will start shouting "Play your songs," stamping their feet, swirling, turning, dancing to the music faster and faster because—

TONIGHT IS CARNAVAL.

When I play my quena with the band, people start to sing. My quena sings and the people sing. I play the special songs I've learned for Carnaval, about llamas, mountains, and friends. We play songs with a beat for dancing. Paco and I watch all the people hold onto each other in one long line that dances—laughing, winding through the village.

Our band plays under the moon and flickering stars, and we will play until the sun comes up. We play the songs of our mountain days and nights . . . for tonight is Carnaval.

HOW ARPILLERAS ARE MADE

An arpillera-maker draws the design on white cloth. Pieces of cloth are selected and cut to fit the design.

Big pieces of cloth are sewn on to form the background.

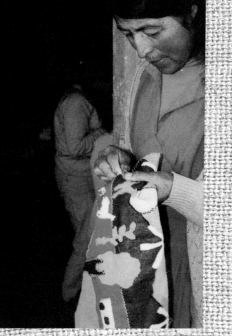

The edges of each shape are neatly stitched, and details are added by sewing on more pieces of cut cloth and by embroidering.

Dolls and other three-dimensional objects (vegetables, musical instruments) are made . . .

Another arpillera is finished.

. . . and sewn onto the arpillera.

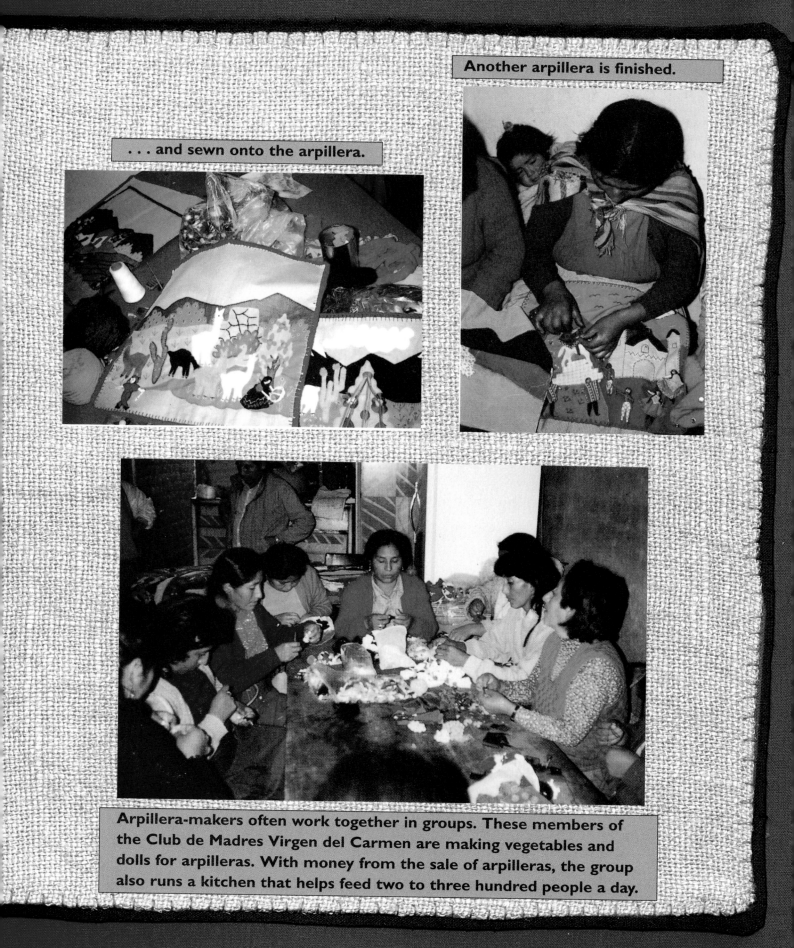

Arpillera-makers often work together in groups. These members of the Club de Madres Virgen del Carmen are making vegetables and dolls for arpilleras. With money from the sale of arpilleras, the group also runs a kitchen that helps feed two to three hundred people a day.

CARNIVAL

In 1885, a newspaper reporter was visiting Saint Paul, Minnesota. He took one look at all the snow, felt the icy wind blowing, and wrote, "No right-minded person would ever come here in the winter!" The people of Saint Paul decided to prove that reporter wrong. Every winter, MILLIONS of visitors flock to the snowy city. What's the attraction? Saint Paul's Winter Carnival, of course! It's the nation's oldest winter carnival, first held in 1886. And it's so much fun that no one even notices the cold!

The giant ice palace is always a favorite with Winter Carnival visitors. It took several weeks and 30,000 huge blocks of ice to build this sparkling castle.

IN THE SNOW

▲ Even a reindeer visited Saint Paul's first Winter Carnival in 1886.

The Legend of the Winter Carnival

A long, long time ago, Boreas, King of all the Winds, discovered Saint Paul—a beautiful ice-covered city in Minnesota. "This frozen wonderland will be my winter capital!" he declared. To celebrate, King Boreas and his queen held a winter carnival in their new home. There were twelve days of feasting and fun for everyone.

But not everyone was happy about the celebration. Boreas's enemy, Vulcanus, King of Fire, hated ice and snow. "Away with winter!" he bellowed. "It's time for spring!"

Vulcanus and his followers plotted to drive King Boreas out of Saint Paul. On the last day of the carnival, Vulcanus stormed into the Boreas's ice castle. To keep the peace, King Boreas agreed to leave. And so the warmth of springtime returned to Saint Paul. However, each year Boreas returns, and he brings another winter carnival with him!

Speedskating is just one of the fun winter sports that take place during the Winter Carnival.

▲ Artists use chainsaws and
chisels to create fantastic
ice carvings. Over a million
people brave the cold
weather each year to see
the frozen sculptures.

▲ From late January to early February, glistening ice sculptures
turn downtown Saint Paul into a winter wonderland.

THINK ABOUT READING

Answer the questions in the story map.

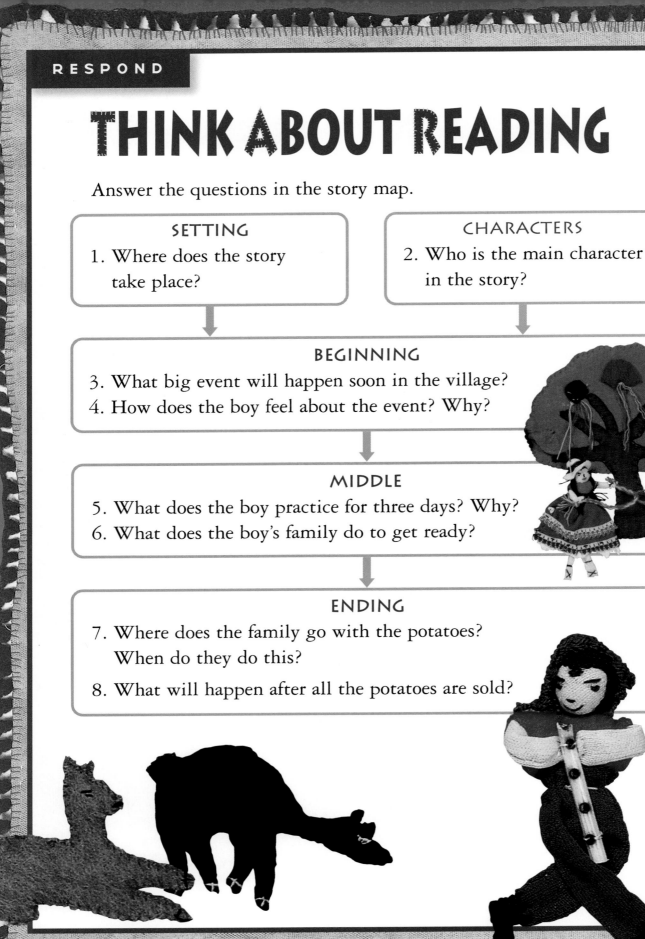

SETTING

1. Where does the story take place?

CHARACTERS

2. Who is the main character in the story?

BEGINNING

3. What big event will happen soon in the village?
4. How does the boy feel about the event? Why?

MIDDLE

5. What does the boy practice for three days? Why?
6. What does the boy's family do to get ready?

ENDING

7. Where does the family go with the potatoes? When do they do this?
8. What will happen after all the potatoes are sold?

WRITE A NEWSPAPER ARTICLE

Community festivals are big news. Write a short newspaper article about the festival in Peru or the one in Saint Paul. Be sure to give all the facts. Tell who or what the article is about. Tell when, where, and why the festival takes place. Be sure to include some colorful details in your article.

LITERATURE CIRCLE

Tonight Is Carnaval and "Carnival in the Snow" both tell about an important community event. How is each story told? What kinds of illustrations does each author use? Tell which methods you liked better, and why. List your ideas on a chart.

AUTHOR
ARTHUR DORROS

Arthur Dorros worked as a house builder, a photographer, and a teacher before he became a children's book author. He likes to travel and learn about other cultures. After living in South America for a year, he wrote *Tonight Is Carnaval*. His advice to young readers is this: "Do what you like, and don't give up."

MORE BOOKS BY
ARTHUR DORROS

- *Abuela*
- *Ant Cities*
- *Rain Forest Secrets*

How to Make a Public-Service Poster

community group's project

Communities are always trying to improve themselves. Some have cleanup days. Others plant community gardens. How do communities advertise projects or events like these? One way is to make public-service posters.

What is a public-service poster? A public-service poster is a large printed sign. It has information about a public concern or event. It may be colorfully illustrated.

Interested in joining...

Linden Heights Neighborhood Garden?

Find out how...

Come to a garden planning meeting
Thursday, July 6
St. Anthony School Cafeteria
6:30 - 7:00 p.m.

Sponsored by:
Grow With Your Neighbors
of Wegerzyn Horticultural Center
S.E. Priority Board
Linden Heights Community Council
City of Dayton, Dept. of Planning

• the event that is being advertised

• place

• time

• organization that made the poster

• colorful decorations

1 Choose an Event

Form a group with several classmates. Decide on an event that will help your community. The event can be a real one that happens in your school or town. It can also be an event that you would like to see happen.

Here are different community events.

- festivals
- cleanup campaigns
- bake sales
- canned-food drives

2 Design the Poster

Your group has chosen an event to announce. Now you can design your poster.

- Decide what you want the poster to say.
- Figure out how it will look. What pictures do you want to go with the words?
- What colors do you want to use?

On a sheet of paper, make a sketch of your design. Do you have all the information you need? Do you like the way it looks?

3 Make a Poster

Now you can make your public-service poster. Decide who will write the words and who will draw the pictures. Remember, neatness counts! When you have finished, take a close look. Are all the words spelled correctly? Have you included the time and place?

Tip A public-service poster may tell community members what they need to bring to an event.

4 Show and Tell

Display your poster in your classroom. Answer any questions your classmates have. Look at their posters, too. How many different kinds of events are advertised? Which events do you think are important?

If You Are Using a Computer . . .

Create your poster on the computer, using borders and clip art. Remember to experiment with font size and style to make your poster look great.

THINK

People do all kinds of things to help their communities. What kinds of things would you like to do?

Lorka Muñoz
Community Garden Director ▶

JAPANESE
FOLK TALE

AWARD
WINNER

THE WISE OLD WOMAN

retold by
Yoshiko Uchida
illustrated by
Martin Springett

Long ago in the wooded hills of Japan, a young farmer and his aged mother lived in a village ruled by a cruel young lord.

"Anyone over seventy is no longer useful," the lord declared, "and must be taken into the mountains and left to die."

When the young farmer's mother reached the dreaded age, he could not bear to think of what he must do. But his mother spoke the words he could not say.

"It is time now for you to take me into the mountains," she said softly.

So, early the next morning, the farmer lifted his mother to his back and reluctantly set off up the steep mountain path.

p and up he climbed—until the trees hid the sun, and the path was gone, until he could no longer hear the birds, but only the sound of the wind shivering through the trees.

On and on he climbed. But soon he heard his mother breaking off small twigs from the trees they passed.

"I'm marking the path for you, my son," she said, "so you will not lose your way going home."

The young farmer could bear it no longer.

other, I cannot leave you behind in the mountains," he said. "We are going home together, and I will never, ever leave you."

And so, in the dark shadows of night, the farmer carried his mother back home. He dug a deep cave beneath the kitchen, and from that day, the old woman lived in this secret room, spinning and weaving. In this way two years passed, and no one in the village knew of the farmer's secret.

Then one day, three fierce warriors in full armor galloped into the small village like a sudden mountain storm.

"We come from the mighty Lord Higa to warn you," they shouted to the young lord. "When three suns have set and three moons have risen, he will come to conquer your village."

T he cruel young lord was not very brave. "Please," he begged, "I will do anything if you will spare me."

"Lord Higa knows no mercy," the warriors thundered, "but he does respect a clever mind. Solve the three impossible tasks written upon this scroll and you and your village will be saved."

Then, tossing the scroll at the young lord, they galloped off as quickly as they had come.

F irst, make a coil of rope out of ashes," the young lord read. "Second, run a single thread through the length of a crooked log. And third, make a drum that sounds without being beaten."

The young lord quickly gathered the six wisest people of his village and ordered them to solve the impossible tasks. They put their heads together and pondered through the night. But when the stars had vanished and the roosters began to crow, they still had no answers for the young lord.

They hurried to the village shrine and sounded the giant bronze bell. "Help us," they pleaded to the gods. But the gods remained silent.

hey went next to seek the clever badger of the forest, for they knew that animals are sometimes wiser than men.

"Surely, you can help us," they said eagerly.

But the badger only shook his head. "As clever as I am," he said, "I see no way to solve such impossible tasks as these."

When the six wise people returned to the young lord without any answers, he exploded in anger.

"You are all stupid fools!" he shouted, and he threw them into his darkest dungeon. Then he posted a sign in the village square offering a bag of gold to anyone who could help him.

The young farmer hurried home to tell his mother about the impossible tasks and Lord Higa's threat. "What are we to do?" he asked sadly. "We will soon be conquered by yet another cruel lord."

The old woman thought carefully and then asked her son to bring her a coil of rope, a crooked log with a hole running through the length of it, and a small hand drum. When the farmer had done as she asked, she set to work.

F irst, she soaked the coil of rope in salt water and dried it well. Then, setting a match to it, she let it burn. But it did not crumble. It held its shape.

"There," she said. "This is your rope of ash."

Next she put a little honey at one end of the crooked log, and at the other, she placed an ant with a silk thread tied to it. The farmer watched in amazement as the tiny ant wound its way through the hole to get to the honey, taking the silk thread with it. And the second task was done.

Finally, the old woman opened one side of the small hand drum and sealed a bumblebee inside. As the bee beat itself against the sides of the drum trying to escape, the drum sounded without being beaten. And the third task was done.

hen the farmer presented the three completed tasks to the young lord, he was astonished. "Surely a young man such as you could not be wiser than the wisest people of our village," he said. "Tell me, what person of wisdom helped you solve these impossible tasks?"

The young farmer could not lie, and he told the lord how he had kept his mother hidden for the past two years. "It is she who solved each of your tasks and saved our village from Lord Higa," he explained.

The farmer waited to be thrown into the dungeon for disobeying the lord. But instead of being angry, the young lord was silent and thoughtful.

I have been wrong," he said at last. "Never again will I send our old people into the mountains to die. Henceforth they will be treated with respect and honor, and will share with us the wisdom of their years."

Whereupon the young lord freed everyone in his dungeon. Next he summoned the old woman and gave her three bags of gold for saving the village.

Finally he allowed the farmer to march with his finest warriors to Lord Higa's castle.

The long procession wound slowly over the mountain roads carrying its precious cargo. And it was the young farmer who carried the lord's banner fluttering high in the autumn wind.

When they presented to Lord Higa the rope of ash and the threaded log and the drum that sounded without being beaten, he stroked his chin thoughtfully.

"I see there is much wisdom in your small village," he said, "for you have solved three truly impossible tasks. Go home," he directed the young farmer, "and tell your lord that his people deserve to live in peace."

From that day on, Lord Higa never threatened the small village again. The villagers prospered, and the young farmer and his mother lived in peace and plenty for all the days of their lives.

FROM The Children's Book of Virtues
EDITED BY William J. Bennett ILLUSTRATED BY Michael Hague

The Little Hero of Holland

Here is the true story of a brave heart, one willing to hold on as long as it takes to get the job done.

Holland is a country where much of the land lies below sea level. Only great walls called dikes keep the North Sea from rushing in and flooding the land. For centuries the people of Holland have worked to keep the walls strong so that their country will be safe and dry. Even the little children know the dikes must be watched every moment, and that a hole no larger than your finger can be a very dangerous thing.

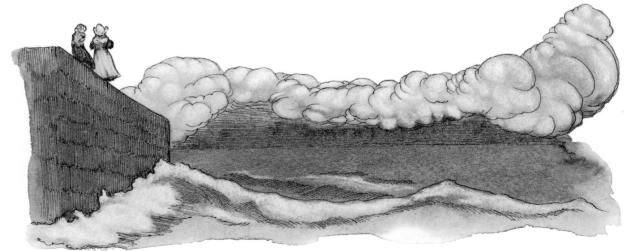

Many years ago there lived in Holland a boy named
Peter. Peter's father was one of the men who tended the
gates in the dikes, called sluices. He opened and closed
the sluices so that ships could pass out of Holland's canals
into the great sea.

One afternoon in the early fall, when Peter was eight
years old, his mother called him from his play. "Come,
Peter," she said. "I want you to go across the dike and take
these cakes to your friend, the blind man. If you go
quickly, and do not stop to play, you will be home again
before dark."

The little boy was glad to go on such an errand, and
started off with a light heart. He stayed with the poor
blind man a little while to tell him about his walk along
the dike and about the sun and the flowers and the ships
far out at sea. Then he remembered his mother's wish that
he should return before dark and, bidding his friend goodbye, he set out for home.

As he walked beside the canal, he noticed how the rains had swollen the waters, and how they beat against the side of the dike, and he thought of his father's gates.

"I am glad they are so strong," he said to himself. "If they gave way what would become of us? These pretty fields would be covered with water. Father always calls them the 'angry waters.' I suppose he thinks they are angry at him for keeping them out so long."

As he walked along he sometimes stopped to pick the pretty blue flowers that grew beside the road, or to listen to the rabbits' soft tread as they rustled through the grass. But oftener he smiled as he thought of his visit to the poor blind man who had so few pleasures and was always so glad to see him.

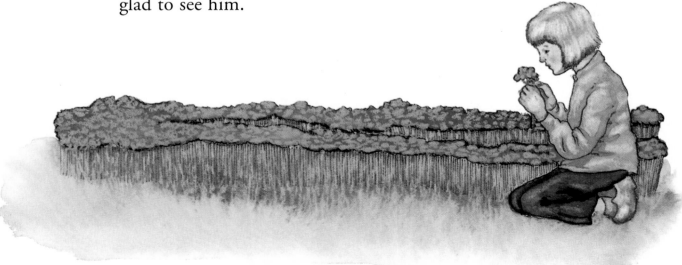

Suddenly he noticed that the sun was setting, and that it was growing dark. "Mother will be watching for me," he thought, and he began to run toward home.

Just then he heard a noise. It was the sound of trickling water! He stopped and looked down. There was a small hole in the dike, through which a tiny stream was flowing.

Any child in Holland is frightened at the thought of a leak in the dike.

Peter understood the danger at once. If the water ran through a little hole it would soon make a larger one, and the whole country would be flooded. In a moment he saw what he must do. Throwing away his flowers, he climbed down the side of the dike and thrust his finger into the tiny hole.

The flowing of the water was stopped!

"Oho!" he said to himself. "The angry waters must stay back now. I can keep them back with my finger. Holland shall not be drowned while I am here."

This was all very well at first, but it soon grew dark and cold. The little fellow shouted and screamed. "Come here; come here," he called. But no one heard him; no one came to help him.

It grew still colder, and his arm ached, and began to grow stiff and numb. He shouted again, "Will no one come? Mother! Mother!"

But his mother had looked anxiously along the dike road many times since sunset for her little boy, and now she had closed and locked the cottage door, thinking that Peter was spending the night with his blind friend, and that she would scold him in the morning for staying away from home without her permission.

Peter tried to whistle, but his teeth chattered with the cold. He thought of his brother and sister in their warm beds, and of his dear father and mother. "I must not let them be drowned," he thought. "I must stay here until someone comes, if I have to stay all night."

The moon and the stars looked down on the child crouching on a stone on the side of the dike. His head was bent, and his eyes were closed, but he was not asleep, for every now and then he rubbed the hand that was holding back the angry sea.

"I'll stand it somehow," he thought. So he stayed there all night keeping the water out.

Early the next morning a man going to work thought he heard a groan as he walked along the top of the dike. Looking over the edge, he saw a child clinging to the side of the great wall.

"What's the matter?" he called. "Are you hurt?"

"I'm keeping the water back!" Peter yelled. "Tell them to come quickly!"

The alarm was spread. People came running with shovels, and the hole was soon mended.

They carried Peter home to his parents, and before long the whole town knew how he had saved their lives that night. To this day, they have never forgotten the brave little hero of Holland.

THINK ABOUT READING

Answer the questions in the story map.

CHARACTERS
1. Who are the three main characters in the story?

SETTING
2. When and where does the story take place?

BEGINNING
3. Why does the farmer take his mother to the mountains?
4. What happens to the mother?

MIDDLE
5. What problem does the young lord face?
6. How does the farmer's mother help?

ENDING
7. How does the young lord act when he finds out what the old woman did?
8. What does the young lord say about old people at the end of the story? Why?

WRITE A BOOK ADVERTISEMENT

Everyone should read *The Wise Old Woman*! Write an advertisement that will persuade third graders to buy this book. Tell why this book is a real winner. Spotlight the brave characters, the exciting plot, and the colorful setting. Be sure to mention the illustrations.

LITERATURE CIRCLE

Talk about the farmer's mother in *The Wise Old Woman* and the boy in *The Little Hero of Holland*. How are these characters alike? How are they different? Show your ideas on a Venn diagram.

AUTHOR
Yoshiko Uchida

Yoshiko Uchida wrote her first stories on brown wrapping paper when she was only ten. She also kept a journal about her life in northern California during the 1930s. Luckily, Ms. Uchida saved these early writings. They helped her create several award-winning books based on her childhood. She has published 28 books including many collections of Japanese folk tales.

More Books by Yoshiko Uchida

- *The Best Bad Thing*
- *The Bracelet*
- *The Dancing Kettle and Other Japanese Folk Tales*

from
...IF YOUR NAME WAS CHANGED
at
Ellis Island

by Ellen Levine

illustrated by Wayne Parmenter

From 1892 to 1924, over twelve million immigrants came to the United States from Europe. For most of these newcomers, Ellis Island was the first stop in America. This immigration center was located in New York harbor. Doctors and legal inspectors checked all the immigrants. A few unlucky ones were sent home. But most entered the United States, and many became American citizens.

Why did people come to America?

Many people believed that America was a "Golden Land"—a place where you could get a decent job, go to a free school, and eat well. There was a saying in Polish that people came to America *za chlebem*—"for bread." One person added that they came "for bread, with butter."

In Russia, six-year-old Alec Bodanis was told that in America, "you'll become a millionaire in no time. Take a shovel with you because they shovel gold from the streets." No one knows how these stories began, but Margot Matyshek, age eleven when she left Germany, had also heard that in America, "the streets are paved with gold. And if you wish for candy, it drops from the sky right into your mouth!"

Some people came to look for work. Wages were higher in America than in their home countries. Until the late 1800s, businesses often sent agents overseas to encourage workers to migrate. If you agreed to work for their companies, they would pay your way to America.

Many people came because land was cheap and plentiful. In 1862, the U.S. government passed a law

called the Homestead Act. Newcomers could stake
a claim to 160 acres of land. After five years of living
on and working the land, they'd pay a small amount
of money, and the acres would be theirs. Railroad
companies also owned a great deal of land in the
west. They sent agents to foreign countries offering
this land for sale at good prices.

Some governments of the new western states
advertised in European newspapers about their growing
towns and cheap farmland. They wanted new settlers.
Often the advertisements were not true. They showed
pictures of towns that didn't exist, and gave descriptions
of farm fields where forests stood. But people came
anyway. Searching, always searching, for a better life.

A Swedish song had these words about America:

> "Ducks and chickens rain right down,
> A roasted goose flies in,
> And on the table lands one more
> with knife and fork stuck in."

Who could find a better place?

What did people bring with them?

Usually whatever they could carry. Some had suitcases and trunks. Most had bundles tied together with string. People carried baskets, cardboard boxes, tins, leather sacks—any type of container you could imagine.

They often brought their feather quilts, mattresses, and pillows, for the steamships just provided thin blankets. They packed fancy clothes, specially embroidered and crocheted. Sometimes people wore layers of all their clothing so they wouldn't have to pack them. Often they brought food for the long trip over the ocean, like smoked sausages or hams, or other foods they thought they couldn't get in America.

Many people had to sell or give away almost everything they owned in order to travel to the new land. But sometimes they were able to bring their favorite things. One young girl mailed her dolls to her relatives in America before she herself came. Another brought a book of fairy tales, which she carried in a basket she held tightly for the whole trip.

How long would the ocean trip take?

Until the mid-1800s, most people came to America on sailing ships. These usually took about forty days to cross the Atlantic Ocean, but sometimes it could take up to six months. By the late 1800s, steamships had replaced sailing ships, and the trip was much faster. If there were no bad storms or other problems, the trip usually took anywhere from six to thirty-two days.

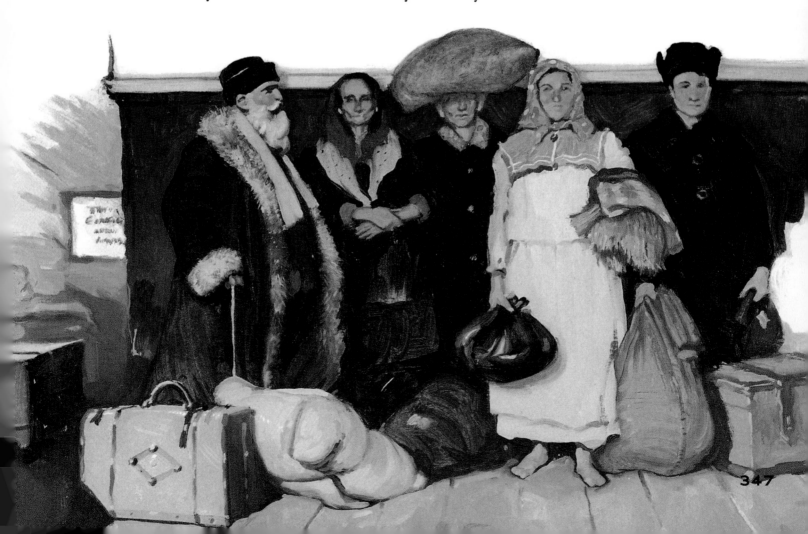

Where would you go when you landed at Ellis Island?

When the barge pulled up to the dock at Ellis Island, immigrants walked under the entry arches into the ground-floor baggage room where some left their luggage. Others held on to all their bags. One baggage worker said he could recognize what country people had come from by the type of luggage they carried and by the way they tied the knots around their bundles.

Then they went up a staircase into the Registry Room, also known as the Great Hall. There they would be examined again by doctors and then by immigration inspectors.

As they reached the top of the stairs, the Great Hall spread out before them like a huge maze. Metal pipes divided the space into narrow aisles, and sections were enclosed in wire mesh. One young immigrant said, "You think you're in a zoo!" After 1911, the iron pipes were removed and replaced by long rows of wooden benches.

Hundreds, at times thousands, of immigrants passed through the Great Hall. The noise, some said, was like the Tower of Babel—sometimes thirty languages being spoken at the same time.

Ellis Island was like a miniature city for immigrants. There were waiting rooms, dormitories for over a thousand people, restaurants, a hospital, baggage room, post office, banks to change foreign money, a railroad ticket office, medical and legal examination rooms, baths, laundries, office areas for charities and church groups, and courtrooms.

Ellis Island was the last hurdle you had to pass before you were to enter the country.

What contributions have immigrants made?

From the time of America's founding, new immigrants have played an important role. Eight of the fifty-five men who signed the Declaration of Independence were born in other countries. And when Thomas Jefferson wrote in the Declaration that "all men are created equal," he used the words of his Italian-born friend Philip Mazzei.

History books often list famous Americans who were immigrants. These lists usually include Albert Einstein, the German-Jewish scientist; Alexander Graham Bell, from Scotland, who invented the telephone; Elizabeth Blackwell, English-born, the first woman doctor in America; Knute Rockne, the Norwegian football player and coach; Marcus Garvey, from Jamaica, the leader of the Back-to-Africa movement; Greta Garbo, the Swedish movie star; Spyros Skouras, the Greek movie producer; Irving Berlin, the Russian-Jewish composer and songwriter; Enrico Fermi, the Italian scientist, and many others.

But millions of immigrants, not just the "famous" ones, created or started things that we think of as totally American. We take these things for granted, but they are the contributions of immigrants:

—log cabins first built by Swedes;

—symphony orchestras and glee clubs organized by Germans;

—movies produced in America by Russian Jews and Greeks;

—Santa Claus, bowling, and ice-skating from the Dutch.

Many peoples contributed to American English. "Yankee" is a Dutch word, and "alligator" is Spanish. "Phooey" is from German, and "prairie" is French. "Jukebox" is African, and "gung ho" is Chinese. And there are hundreds more words that were originally foreign and are now part of the English language.

If you think of Native American Indians as the first immigrants, then the names of many states come from Indian "immigrant" languages: Arizona, Wisconsin, Wyoming, Connecticut, Mississippi, and Oklahoma, to name a few. "Raccoon," "skunk," and "succotash" also are Indian words.

As Abraham Lincoln said, immigrants have been "a source of national wealth and strength."

This Land Is Your Land

WORDS AND MUSIC BY WOODY GUTHRIE
ARRANGED BY JAMES ROOKER

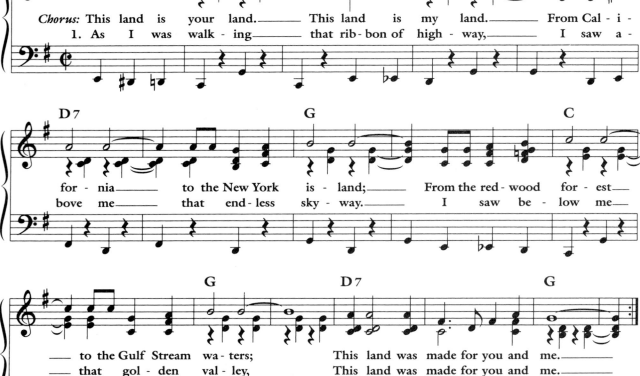

2. I've roamed and rambled and I followed my footsteps
To the sparkling sands of her diamond deserts,
And all around me a voice was sounding,
"This land was made for you and me."

Chorus

3. When the sun comes shining and I was strolling
And the wheat fields waving and the dust clouds rolling,
As the fog was lifting a voice was chanting,
"This land was made for you and me."

Chorus

Miss Liberty Celebration. Malcah Zeldis
The National Museum of American Art, Smithsonian Institution

Think About Reading

Write your answers.

1. Why did immigrants want to come to America?

2. How do you think immigrants felt when they walked into the Great Hall at Ellis Island? Why?

3. Imagine that you were an immigrant coming to America a hundred years ago. How would you feel about leaving your home and traveling to a new country?

4. How does the author present information about Ellis Island?

5. What does the song "This Land Is Your Land" tell immigrants about America?

Write an Account

Imagine that you are an immigrant coming to America in the early 1900s. You have just arrived at Ellis Island. Write about your experiences. How do you feel when you step off the boat? What do you see? What do you hear? Use details to help your reader picture what happened to you.

Literature Circle

Immigrants have added a lot to American life. Talk about the contributions you think are important. Tell why you think so. Record your ideas on a chart.

AUTHOR
Ellen Levine

Reading and learning are adventures for author Ellen Levine. In fact, she began writing nonfiction books so that she could share the excitement of learning with children. She interviewed hundreds of people and read many old journals and letters before she wrote . . .*If Your Name Was Changed at Ellis Island.* This talented author has also been a teacher, a film producer, and a cartoonist.

More Books by Ellen Levine

- *The Tree That Would Not Die*
- *. . .If You Traveled on the Underground Railroad*
- *I Hate English!*

How to Make a Community Recipe Book

How do people in communities learn about each other? One way is by sharing favorite foods. Some communities even put together community recipe books. The recipe books may contain old recipes, recipes from other countries, or family favorites.

What is a recipe book? A recipe book contains a collection of recipes for foods. A recipe is a list of ingredients and directions for making a food or drink.

- title of recipe tells the kind of food you are making

Family Biscuits

2 cups all-purpose flour
1 tablespoon baking powder
1 teaspoon salt
1/3 cup shortening
3/4 cup milk

- ingredients you need to make the food

1. Heat oven to 425°F.

2. Combine flour, baking powder and salt in large bowl. Mix in shortening until it forms coarse crumbs. Add milk. Mix with fork. Form dough into ball.

- directions for putting the ingredients together

3. Put dough on lightly floured surface. Knead gently 8 to 10 times. Roll dough to 1/2-inch thickness. Cut with floured 2-inch round cutter. Place on ungreased baking sheet.

4. Bake at 425°F for 12 to 14 minutes.

Makes 12 to 16 biscuits.

- a paragraph that tells why this food is important to you

YOU MIGHT MAKE A FRIEND ALONG THE WAY

When I was about 7 or 8 years old, I'd come home from school and find my grandmother baking those delicious oversized biscuits. A platter of them would be on top of the stove to keep warm. I'd sneak up to the stove and grab a biscuit then run outside to play. She always caught me, pulled me back by my shirttail and said, "Where are you going?" I'd tell her I was going outside to play. Then she would hand me another biscuit and say, "You'd better take two because you might make a friend along the way."

Phil Mendez
Los Angeles, CA

1   Choose a Recipe

Think of a special food that you like—one that you want to share with your classmates. It might be a recipe that has been in your family for years. You might eat it only on holidays or special occasions. Or it might be a food that your family likes and prepares often. Bring the recipe to class.

TOOLS

- paper and pencil
- colored pencils or marking pens

Here are some different kinds of foods to choose recipes for:

- salads
- breads
- vegetables
- meat or fish dishes
- pasta
- desserts

2   Talk Food

Now you have a recipe. Write a few sentences telling why it is important to you. You may have a happy memory about this food. If it's a holiday food, there may be a story that goes with it. The food may remind you of a special person you know.

3 Write the Recipe

Now you are ready to copy your recipe and your story about it onto a clean sheet of paper. Write down the ingredients and directions carefully. Make sure you have copied everything correctly so that the recipe will come out right. Include your story and write your name at the bottom.

You may wish to decorate your recipe.

Tip Some recipes need special cooking tools. Be sure you include these tools in your recipe's directions.

4 It's a Book!

Put all the recipes together to make your community recipe book. Work with your classmates to design a cover. You may want to group similar recipes together. When you have finished, talk about the recipes in your book. Which ones do you know? Which ones are new? Which ones would you like to try?

If You Are Using a Computer . . .

Draft your recipe on the computer and decorate it with a special border. You also can create a table of contents for your cookbook on the computer.

THINK

Everyone in a community has different ideas. Why do you think sharing recipes and food is a good way to bring members of a community together?

Lorka Muñoz
Community Garden Director ▶

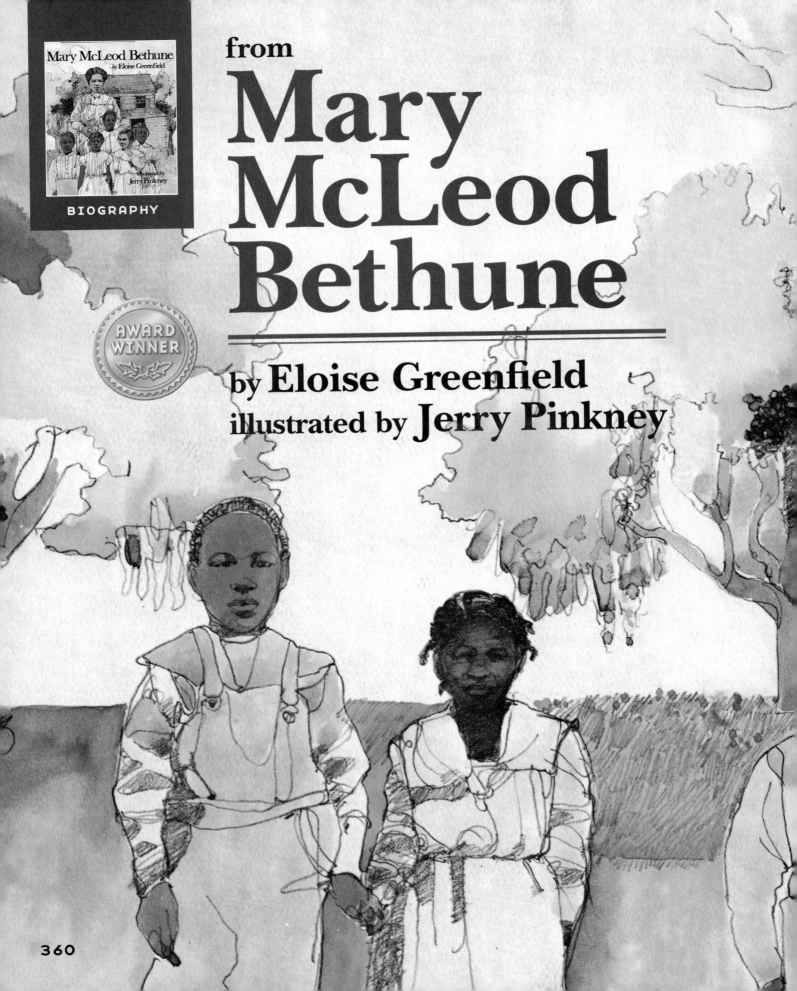

from

Mary McLeod Bethune

by **Eloise Greenfield**
illustrated by **Jerry Pinkney**

As a child, Mary McLeod Bethune dreamed of going to school and learning to read. She finally got her chance in 1886, when she was 11 years old. Emma Wilson and Lucy Laney, both teachers, helped Mary make her dream come true. Once Mary Bethune was on her way, she kept right on going until she became a teacher, too.

A few years after she began teaching, Mary met Albertus Bethune, also a teacher, who became her husband. The following year, their son, Albert, was born.

When Albert was five years old, Mary Bethune made a big decision. She wanted to start a school of her own. She thought of Miss Laney and Miss Wilson, and she remembered herself as a child longing to learn. There were many black children like her who lived in places without schools. They had questions but no answers. They wanted to learn and she wanted to teach them.

She heard about Daytona Beach, Florida, where a new railroad was being built. The workmen who were putting down the railroad track were not being paid enough. They lived with their families in camps that were too crowded. There were no schools. Mrs. Bethune decided that she would go there.

When Mrs. Bethune arrived in Daytona Beach, she had only one dollar and fifty cents. She stayed with a friend, and every day she went for a walk, looking for a building that she could use as a school. Finally, she found an old two-story cottage. The owner said he would rent it to her for eleven dollars a month. He agreed to wait a few weeks until she could raise the first month's rent.

Mrs. Bethune visited the homes of black families, telling them about her school. Neighbors came to paint the cottage and to fix the broken steps. Children helped with the cleaning.

On an autumn day in 1904, Mrs. Bethune stood in the doorway of the cottage, smiling and ringing a bell. It was time for school to start. Five little girls came in and took their seats. The school was named the Daytona Normal and Industrial School for Girls. It was an elementary school, and Albert would learn there, too, until he was older.

Mrs. Bethune and the students used wooden boxes as desks and chairs. They burned logs and used the charcoal as pencils. They mashed berries and used the juice as ink.

The children loved the school. Some of them lived there with Mrs. Bethune. All of them wanted to help raise money for the rent and for the books and paper and lamps and beds that they needed.

After classes, they made ice cream and pies to sell. The children peeled and mashed sweet potatoes while Mrs. Bethune rolled the crust. They gave programs at hotels and in churches. The children sang and recited. Mrs. Bethune spoke to the audiences about the school. She bought a secondhand bicycle and rode all over Daytona Beach, knocking on doors and asking people for their help.

Many people gave. Some of them were rich, and some of them did not have much money themselves but were willing to share the little that they had.

When too many children wanted to attend and a larger building was needed, adults in the community again gave their time and work. They took away the trash from the land that Mrs. Bethune bought. Those who were carpenters helped to put the building up. Those who were gardeners planted flowers and trees around it.

Mrs. Bethune named the new building Faith Hall in honor of her favorite building at Scotia Seminary. She had faith in God, in herself, and in black people. Over the door she hung a sign that said "Enter to learn."

Across from Faith Hall, Mrs. Bethune started a small farm. The students planted fruits and vegetables to use and to sell. They grew strawberries, tomatoes, string beans, carrots, and corn. They grew sugar cane to make syrup.

As the years passed, more students came to the school, and more teachers. More buildings were added. Albert went away to school, but Mrs. Bethune was busier than ever. Almost every day a new problem arose that she had to solve.

One day, a student became very ill. Because there was no hospital for blacks for many, many miles, Mrs. Bethune rushed her to the nearest white hospital. The doctors agreed to take care of her, but not inside the hospital. They put the patient on the back porch with a screen around her bed.

Mrs. Bethune was very angry, but there was nothing she could do. The student was too sick to be moved to another hospital. But when the girl was well, Mrs. Bethune decided that someone had to start a hospital for blacks in Daytona Beach, and she would do it. She started a little two-bed hospital which later had twenty beds. She named it McLeod Hospital in memory of her father, who had died. It saved many black lives.

Later that same year, one of Mrs. Bethune's brothers came for his first visit. He walked around the campus with his sister and visited classrooms where young people were being taught to use their minds and their hands. The choir sang for him. He was proud of his sister and of all that he saw and heard, and Mrs. Bethune was proud to show him what had been done.

POEM

RUSHING

IN TWIRLS

COILING

LEAP

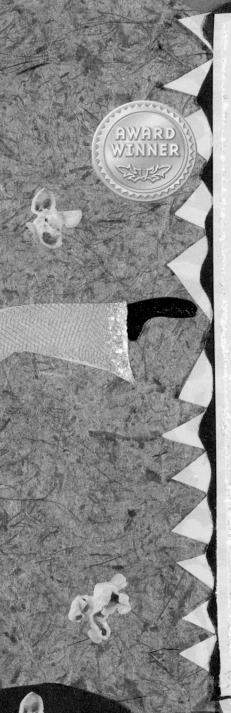

I Love the Look of Words

by Maya Angelou

Popcorn leaps, popping from the floor
of a hot black skillet
and into my mouth.
Black words leap,
snapping from the white
page. Rushing into my eyes. Sliding
into my brain which gobbles them
the way my tongue and teeth
chomp the buttered popcorn.

When I have stopped reading,
ideas from the words stay stuck
in my mind, like the sweet
smell of butter perfuming my
fingers long after the popcorn
is finished.

I love the book and the look of words
the weight of ideas that popped into my mind
I love the tracks
of new thinking in my mind.

Think About Reading

Write your answers.

1. Why did Mary McLeod Bethune move to Daytona Beach?

2. What kind of person was Mrs. Bethune? How do you know?

3. Imagine you could go back in time to Mrs. Bethune's school. What questions would you like to ask her students?

4. How does the author feel about Mary McLeod Bethune? How can you tell?

5. How might Mrs. Bethune feel about the poem "I Love the Look of Words"?

Write a Speech

Mrs. Bethune made speeches to people in the community about her school. What do you think she might have said? Write a short speech for Mrs. Bethune. Try to convince her listeners that they should help the school. Tell what needs to be done and why.

Literature Circle

Suppose you could talk to author Eloise Greenfield. What questions would you ask her about writing or about Mary McLeod Bethune? How might she answer them?

Author
Eloise Greenfield

Eloise Greenfield never dreamed she would be a poet and author. She says, "I loved words, but I loved to *read* them, not *write* them." Then she came down with a severe case of "word-madness" in the 1970s. Since then she has written poems, stories, and biographies that help children feel good about themselves. Like Mary McLeod Bethune, Eloise Greenfield wants to make life better for friends, neighbors, and family.

More Books by
Eloise Greenfield

- *Africa Dream*
- *Under the Sunday Tree*
- *For the Love of the Game: Michael Jordan and Me*

How to
Create a Community Quilt

Design a quilt that tells all about your community.

Have you ever seen a community quilt? It's a special patchwork wall hanging that celebrates the good things about a community. On a community quilt you may see pictures of famous landmarks, community events, beautiful parks, or important people. You may even find words written on it. Many of these special quilts are beautiful works of art. But they also show why communities are great places to live.

Kevin

Age 8

HAPPY BIRTHDAY AMERICA

Wendy

Age 8

Michael

Age 6

1976

Katie

Age 7

Mike

Age 6

1 Choose a Subject

With your classmates, list the things that make your community unlike any other. These may include people, places, events, or activities. Choose the part of your community that you want to show on a quilt square.

Special parts of your community might be:

- famous landmarks such as statues or buildings
- city, state, or national parks
- community groups
- places that people use, such as libraries or playfields
- celebrations and parades
- people, such as the mayor

TOOLS

- paper and pencil
- squares of colored construction paper
- glue
- colored pencils, crayons, marking pens, or paint
- scissors

2 **Research It**

Find out something about the landmark, place, group, person, or activity you have chosen. You can look for information in your school or local library. You can talk to people who have lived in the community for a long time. You can call or write to your local chamber of commerce, too. If you are researching a place, you may be able to visit it. Take notes on the information you find.

Here are some questions you can ask about a landmark, place, or event:

- How long has it been in the community?

- What is it? What does it do?

- Why is it important?

Now you're ready to design your quilt square for your community quilt.

How Am I Doing?

Before you make your community quilt, take a few minutes and ask yourself these questions:

- Have I chosen a landmark, place, person, group, or activity that is important to my community?

- Have I found information about my choice?

3

Design Your Square

Decide what your quilt square will look like. On a sheet of construction paper, draw a picture of the person, group, landmark, place, or activity that you have researched.

Around the edges of the paper, glue on a border of a different colored paper. On your square, write the name of your choice. If you want, add an interesting fact about it. Write your name and age below your drawing or on the border.

COUNTY FAIR

Farm Animals

Corn

Pies

Ferris Wheel

Anne Smith   Age 8

OUR TOWN'S

Eve Chin
Age 7

150-YEAR-OLD TREE

Bill Trujillo
Age 8

Tip Make sure all the squares in your community quilt are the same size. That way, they will easily fit together.

4 | Make a Quilt

With your classmates, glue all the quilt squares together. You may want to make several small quilts instead of one large one. Display your quilts on a classroom wall.

Then tell the class what you learned about your community. Answer any questions. Have a quilt party, too! Invite other classes in your school to see your community quilt.

If You Are Using a Computer ...

Work with your classmates to design your quilt on the computer. Use a graphics program that has a background grid. Use the Shape Tools to create individual panels. Then type or draw within the squares to show what will go where. Print out your work to use as a guide when you put the quilt together.

JULY 4th

PARADE

Our Mayor

Town Hall

Sam Wada
Age 7

Mayor Jill Lobo

CONGRATULATIONS

You have learned how people improve their communities. What can you do to make your community a better place?

Lorka Muñoz
Community Garden Director ▶

You will find all your vocabulary words in alphabetical order in the Glossary. Look at the sample entry below to see how to use it.

This is the **entry word** you look up. It is divided into syllables.

This part tells you how to **pronounce** the entry word. It uses the marks in the pronunciation key.

tum·ble·weeds (tum´ bəl wēdz´) *noun*
Bushy plants that grow in the deserts and plains of western North America. In the autumn, the wind breaks *tumbleweeds* off at their roots and blows them around. ▲ **tumbleweed**

tumbleweed

This tells you what **part of speech** the entry word is.

Look here to find the **meaning** of the word. There also may be a sentence that tells more about the word or that shows how the word is used.

This is **another form** of the entry word.

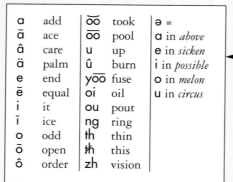

a	add	o͝o	took	ə =		
ā	ace	o͞o	pool	a in *above*		
â	care	u	up	e in *sicken*		
ä	palm	û	burn	i in *possible*		
e	end	yo͞o	fuse	o in *melon*		
ē	equal	oi	oil	u in *circus*		
i	it	ou	pout			
ī	ice	ng	ring			
o	odd	th	thin			
ō	open	ᵺ	this			
ô	order	zh	vision			

The **pronunciation key** will help you figure out how to pronounce the entry word.

a·do·be

(ə dō′ bē) *noun*
A sandy kind of clay used to make bricks. Sometimes bits of straw are mixed with the clay.

ad·ver·tise·ments

(ad′ vər tīz′ mənts) *noun*
Public announcements that describe a product or service for sale. TV and radio commercials are advertisements. Advertisements are also found in newspapers and magazines.
▲ **advertisement**

al·pac·a

(al pak′ ə) *noun*
An animal that has long silky brown or black wool. An alpaca looks like a llama.

an·ces·tor

(an′ ses tər) *noun*
A person, now dead, from whom one is descended. One *ancestor* of mine moved to America from Russia in the late 1800s.

an·cient

(ān′ shənt) *adjective*
Very old or very long ago. These *ancient* toys were made thousands of years ago.

Thesaurus
ancient
old
aged
antique

ar·chae·ol·o·gists

(är′ kē ol′ ə jists) *noun*
People who study the past by digging up old buildings and objects and looking carefully at them. The *archaeologists* discovered an ancient village. ▲ **archaeologist**

artifacts

ar·ti·facts

(är′ tə fakts′) *noun*
Tools or objects made and used by people long ago. The arrowheads were the oldest *artifacts* in the museum.
▲ **artifact**

au·di·enc·es
(ô´ dē ən səz) *noun*
Groups of people
gathered in a place to
hear or see something.
▲ audience

bou·quets
(bō kāz´ *or* bo͞o kāz´)
noun Bunches of cut or
picked flowers. The
girls picked daisies for
their *bouquets.*
▲ bouquet

bouquet

bur·lap
(bûr´ lap) *noun*
A rough brown cloth.
It is used for making
bags and other things.

cactus

cac·tus
(kak´ təs) *noun*
A desert plant that has
a thick stem covered
with sharp spines
instead of leaves.
▲ cacti *or* cactuses

cam·pus
(kam´ pəs) *noun*
The grounds and
buildings of a school,
such as a college.

can·vas
(kan´ vəs) *noun*
A heavy, coarse cloth
used for making tents,
sails, and wagon covers.

case (kās) *noun*
A crime that a detective
or police officer is
investigating.

cat·a·logues
or cat·a·logs
(kat´ əl lôgz) *noun*
Books or pamphlets
listing things you can
buy from a company.
The clothes we ordered
from the *catalogues*
came in the mail.
▲ catalogue *or*
catalog

chimney

chim·ney
(chim´ nē) *noun*
A hollow structure in a
building—often made of
bricks or stones—that
carries away smoke from
a fireplace or furnace.

chi·na
(chī´ nə) *adjective*
Made of fine pottery.

com·pli·cat·ed
(kom´ pli kā´ tid)
adjective Not easy
to understand or do.
The boy couldn't
understand the
complicated directions
for playing the game.

com·put·er
(kəm pyōō´ tər) *noun*
An electronic machine
that stores information
and solves complicated
problems quickly.

con·quer
(kong´ kər) *verb*
To defeat and
take control of
an enemy. The
army will *conquer*
the city.

coy·o·te
(kī ō´ tē *or* kī´ ōt) *noun*
An animal that looks
like a small, thin wolf.
It lives in North
America and is closely
related to wolves,
foxes, and dogs.

computer

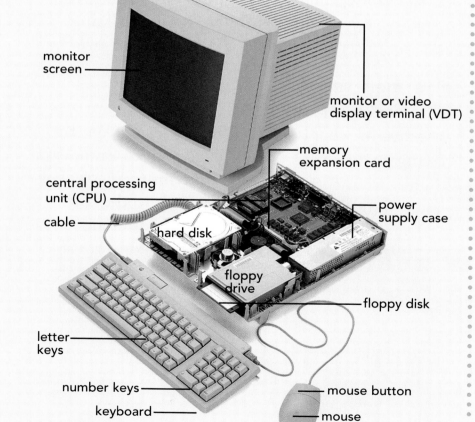

monitor screen

central processing unit (CPU)

cable

hard disk

floppy drive

letter keys

number keys

keyboard

monitor or video display terminal (VDT)

memory expansion card

power supply case

floppy disk

mouse button

mouse

coyote

a	add	ōō	took	ə =
ā	ace	ōō	pool	a in *above*
â	care	u	up	e in *sicken*
ä	palm	û	burn	i in *possible*
e	end	yōō	fuse	o in *melon*
ē	equal	oi	oil	u in *circus*
i	it	ou	pout	
ī	ice	ng	ring	
o	odd	th	thin	
ō	open	ŧħ	this	
ô	order	zh	vision	

dam·age

(dam´ ij) *noun* The harm that something does. The heavy winds caused *damage* to the oak trees.

dem·on·strate

(dem´ ən strāt´) *verb* Show or explain clearly. On Monday, I will *demonstrate* how to use the computer.

des·ert

(dez´ ərt) *noun* A dry, often sandy area where hardly any plants grow because there is so little rain.

de·tec·tive

(di tek´ tiv) *noun* A person who follows clues to solve a crime.

ditch

(dich) *noun* A long, narrow trench that drains water away. The farmer dug a *ditch* in his field.

e·lec·tron·ic

(i lek tron´ ik) *adjective* Having to do with equipment powered by electricity, such as radios, televisions, and computers.

el·e·men·ta·ry

(el´ ə men´ tə rē) *adjective* In school, having to do with kindergarten through grades four, five, or six.

e·mer·gen·cy

(i mûr´ jən sē) *noun* A very sudden and surprising situation that must be handled quickly.

ex·hib·its

(ig zib´ its) *noun* Groups of things that are shown. I saw four *exhibits* of old tools at the history fair.
▲ exhibit

ex·tinct

(ik stingkt´) *adjective* No longer existing. Dinosaurs are *extinct*.

field trip

(fēld´ trip´) *noun* A trip away from the classroom to learn about something. We took a *field trip* to the museum to study dinosaurs.

desert

fierce

(fērs) *adjective*
Frightening and dangerous. The *fierce* bear defended her cubs.

ford (fôrd) *noun*
A shallow place where a river can be crossed.

for·eign

(fôr´ in) *adjective*
From another country. We cooked a dinner of *foreign* foods.

foun·da·tion

(foun dā´ shən) *noun*
The bottom or base of a building, usually below ground. The workers built the new house on top of a stone *foundation.*

WORD HISTORY

The word **foundation** comes from a Latin word that means "bottom." The *foundation* of a building is always on the bottom.

---

gust (gust) *noun*
A sudden, strong blast of wind. The *gust* blew Dad's hat away.

hab·i·tat

(hab´ i tat´) *noun*
The place where an animal or plant naturally lives and grows. A whale's *habitat* is the ocean.

hail (hāl) *noun*
Small balls of ice that fall like rain from the clouds. Rain and icy *hail* beat against the windows during the storm.

har·vest

(här´ vist) *verb*
To gather a crop when it is ripe. The farmer will *harvest* her corn in August.

---

hitched (hicht) *verb*
Tied or fastened with a rope. I hitched the mule to the wagon.
▲ **hitch**

horse·shoe

(hôrs´ sho͞o´) *noun*
A flat, U-shaped metal plate. It is nailed to the bottom of a horse's hoof to protect it.

harvest

a	add	o͝o	took	ə =
ā	ace	o͞o	pool	a in *above*
â	care	u	up	e in *sicken*
ä	palm	û	burn	i in *possible*
e	end	yo͞o	fuse	o in *melon*
ē	equal	oi	oil	u in *circus*
i	it	ou	pout	
ī	ice	ng	ring	
o	odd	th	thin	
ō	open	ŧh	this	
ô	order	zh	vision	

in·spec·tors
(in spek´ tərz) *noun*
People who look over official papers with care. The *inspectors* looked at our passports when we arrived at the airport.
▲ inspector

javelina

ja·ve·li·na
(hä´ və lē´ nə) *noun*
A wild pig that lives in Mexico and the southwestern United States; a peccary.

land·scape
(land´ skāp´) *noun*
A view or scene of surrounding land. The *landscape* was filled with trees and mountains.

leg·end
(lej´ ənd) *noun*
A story that is handed down through the years. Some, or all of the story may not be true.

lla·mas (lä´ məz or yä´ məz) *noun*
South American animals that are related to camels but are smaller and have no humps. Llamas carry heavy loads. Their wool is used for making cloth.
▲ llama

FACT FILE
- When a **llama** gets angry, it spits.
- Llamas have big eyes with long eyelashes that make them look cute.
- Llamas can live in very high places in the mountains.

lot (lot) *noun*
A piece of land. We'll build our house on this *lot*.

lurched (lûrcht) *verb*
Suddenly swayed in one direction or from side to side. The car *lurched* forward and then came to a stop.
▲ lurch

ma·chines
(mə shēnz´) *noun*
Equipment with moving parts used to do special jobs. People use sewing *machines* to make clothes.
▲ machine

llama

mam·moth

(mam´ əth) *noun*
A large animal, like an elephant, that lived long ago. It had shaggy brown hair and long, curved tusks.

orchard

WORD STUDY

The **mammoth** was such a huge animal that people began to use its name to describe something that was large. The word *mammoth* can also mean "huge, gigantic, giant, or very large."

---

man·sion

(man´ shən) *noun*
A very large and elegant home. The *mansion* had 30 rooms and a long driveway.

mi·grate

(mī´ grāt) *verb*
To move from one country to another. Many people from other countries *migrate* to America.

mys·ter·y

(mis´ tə rē *or* mis´ trē) *noun* A story containing a puzzle that has to be solved.

new·com·ers

(no͞o´ kum ərz *or* nyo͞o´ kum ərz) *noun* People who have just arrived in a place. The *newcomers* on my block moved here last month.
▲ **newcomer**

of·fi·cer

(ô´ fə sər) *noun*
A member of a police department. The *officer* solved the crime.

or·chards

(ôr´ chərdz) *noun*
Fields where fruit trees or nut trees are grown. We picked oranges in the *orchards.*
▲ **orchard**

par·tic·i·pants

(pär tis´ ə pənts) *noun*
People who join others in an activity. All the *participants* in the parade wore funny costumes.
▲ **participant**

a	add	o͝o	took	ə =		
ā	ace	o͞o	pool	a in *above*		
â	care	u	up	e in *sicken*		
ä	palm	û	burn	i in *possible*		
e	end	yo͞o	fuse	o in *melon*		
ē	equal	oi	oil	u in *circus*		
i	it	ou	pout			
ī	ice	ng	ring			
o	odd	th	thin			
ō	open	ħ	this			
ô	order	zh	vision			

pray·ing man·tis

(prā´ ing man´ tis) *noun*
An insect with long
stick-like legs and a
triangle-shaped head.
It is related to the
grasshopper.

praying mantis

pre·his·tor·ic

(prē´ hi stôr´ ik)
adjective Belonging
to times before
history was recorded
in writing.
Mammoths lived
in *prehistoric* times.

pre·served

(pri zûrvd´) *verb*
Protected and kept
in an original state.
Some mammoths
were *preserved* in ice.
▲ preserve

pro·ces·sion

(prə sesh´ ən) *noun*
Many people walking
along a street as part
of a festival or parade.
The queen and king
led a *procession* of people
along the main road.

pro·grams

(prō´ gramz) *noun*
Entertainment seen in
theaters, on television,
or heard on the radio.
During the school year,
we gave three musical
programs for our
parents. ▲ program

proj·ect

(proj´ ekt) *noun*
A special study, task, or
activity. I collected sea
shells for my science
project.

pros·pered

(pros´ pərd) *verb*
Was successful and
became wealthy. The
artist *prospered* when she
sold her paintings.
▲ prosper

pueblo

pueb·lo

(pweb´ lō) *noun*
A Native American
village that is made
up of stone or adobe
buildings sometimes
built one above the
other. Pueblos are found
in the southwestern
United States.

WORD HISTORY

The word **pueblo** comes
from a Spanish word
meaning "people" or
"town." Long ago,
Spanish explorers
thought that Native
American adobe villages
in the Southwest
looked like towns in
Spain, so they called
them pueblos. The
Native Americans who
lived in these adobe
villages were also
known as Pueblo
Indians.

re·cit·ed

(ri sī´ tid) *verb*
Spoke from memory in front of a group. Oscar *recited* some poems for his class. ▲ **recite**

re·mem·ber

(ri mem´ bər) *verb*
To bring back to mind. I *remember* my trip to Yellowstone Park last summer.

re·pro·grammed

(rē prō´ gramd) *verb*
Gave new instructions to a computer about how to do its work.
▲ **reprogram**

re·spect

(ri spekt´) *noun*
A feeling of high regard or admiration. I have *respect* for people who tell the truth.

ro·bots

(rō´ bəts or rō´ bots) *noun* Machines that do jobs usually done by people. In the movie, *robots* washed the dishes and cleaned the house. ▲ **robot**

robot

ru·ins

(rōō´ inz) *noun*
Buildings that have fallen apart or have been destroyed. We visited the *ruins* of an old castle on our vacation. ▲ **ruin**

ruins

a	add	ŏŏ	took	ə =
ā	ace	ōō	pool	a in *above*
â	care	u	up	e in *sicken*
ä	palm	û	burn	i in *possible*
e	end	yōō	fuse	o in *melon*
ē	equal	oi	oil	u in *circus*
i	it	ou	pout	
ī	ice	ng	ring	
o	odd	th	thin	
ō	open	ŧh	this	
ô	order	zh	vision	

run·ning gear

(run´ ing gēr´) *noun*
The part of a wagon that the wheels and steering bar are connected to.

scare·crows

(scâr´ krōz´) *noun*
Straw figures dressed like people and put in fields to scare birds away from crops. Birds fly by when they see *scarecrows*.
▲ scarecrow

scarecrow

so·lar

(sō´ lər) *adjective*
Having to do with the sun, as in a *solar* eclipse.

solve (solv) *verb*
To find the answer to a problem or mystery. The detectives will *solve* the crime and catch the criminal.

splash (splash) *verb*
To hit or move through water or other liquids so that they are thrown about.

stalk·ing

(stô´ king) *verb*
Following someone or something so as to get close without being seen. The gray cat was *stalking* a large black beetle. ▲ stalk

stor·y·tel·ler

(stôr´ ē tel´ ər) *noun*
A person who tells or writes stories for fun or learning.

ta·ble (tā´ bəl) *noun*
A piece of furniture with a flat top. It is held up by one or more legs.

WORD HISTORY

The word **table** comes from a Latin word that means "a board." Long ago, people placed things on boards, just as we put things on *tables* today.

teach·ers

(tē´ chərz) *noun*
People who teach in a school or college.
▲ teacher

ter·ra·ces

(ter´ əs əz) *noun*
Flat areas cut out of hills. People often plant flowers or vegetables on *terraces*.
▲ terrace

tor·na·do

(tôr nā´ dō) *noun*
A violent, whirling wind that appears as a dark funnel-shaped cloud. A *tornado* travels at breakneck speed and usually destroys everything in its path. ▲ tornadoes *or* tornados

Thesaurus
tribe
clan
family
kin

tribe (trīb) *noun*
A group of people with the same ancestors, customs, and language. The Hopi are a *tribe* of Native Americans who live in the American Southwest.

FACT FILE

- **Tornadoes** have whirling winds that reach a speed of 200 miles per hour.
- Most tornadoes strike in the midwestern and southern United States.
- Other names for *tornado* are *cyclone* and *twister*.

tum·ble·weeds

(tum´ bəl wēdz) *noun*
Bushy plants that grow in the deserts and plains of western North America. In the fall, the wind breaks *tumbleweeds* off at their roots and blows them around. ▲ tumbleweed

tumbleweed

---

twist·er

(twis´ tər) *noun*
A tornado. The *twister* tore the roof off of the old barn.

twister

war·ri·ors

(wôr´ ē ərz or wôr´ yərz) *noun*
Soldiers, or people experienced in fighting battles. The *warriors* fought until their side won. ▲ warrior

a	add	o͞o	took	ə =
ā	ace	ōo	pool	a in *above*
â	care	u	up	e in *sicken*
ä	palm	û	burn	i in *possible*
e	end	yo͞o	fuse	o in *melon*
ē	equal	oi	oil	u in *circus*
i	it	ou	pout	
ī	ice	ng	ring	
o	odd	th	thin	
ō	open	ŧh	this	
ô	order	zh	vision	

Acknowledgments

Grateful acknowledgment is made to the following sources for permission to reprint from previously published material. The publisher has made diligent efforts to trace the ownership of all copyrighted material in this volume and believes that all necessary permissions have been secured. If any errors or omissions have inadvertently been made, proper corrections will gladly be made in future editions.

Cover, Title Page, and Unit 6 Community Quilt Table of Contents: From TONIGHT IS CARNAVAL by Arthur Dorros, illustrated with arpilleras sewn by the Club de Madres Virgen del Carmen of Lima, Peru. Copyright © 1991 by Dutton Children's Books for illustrations. Used by permission of Dutton Children's Books, a division of Penguin Putnam Inc.

Unit 4 Hit Series: Table of Contents: From THE STORY OF BABAR by Jean de Brunhoff. Copyright © 1962 by Random House, Inc. Reprinted by permission of Random House, Inc. ENCYCLOPEDIA BROWN from ENCYCLOPEDIA BROWN: BOY DETECTIVE by Donald J. Sobol, illustrated by Leonard Shortall. Illustrations copyright © 1974 by Thomas Nelson, Inc. Used by permission of Lodestar Books, an affiliate of Dutton Children's Books, a division of Penguin Putnam Inc. JULIAN illustration from cover of MORE STORIES JULIAN TELLS by Ann Cameron. Illustration copyright © 1986 by Ann Strugnell. Reprinted by permission of Alfred A. Knopf, Inc. KERMIT: Kermit the Frog is copyrighted and used by special permission of Jim Henson Productions. MS. FRIZZLE from THE MAGIC SCHOOL BUS book series by Joanna Cole and Bruce Degen. Copyright © 1993 by Scholastic Productions Inc. All rights reserved. Used by permission.

Unit 4 Hit Series:
Unit Opener: From THE STORY OF BABAR by Jean de Brunhoff. Copyright © 1962 by Random House, Inc. Reprinted by permission of Random House, Inc. BATMAN image property of DC Comics. Used by permission. BATMAN is a trademark of DC Comics copyright © 1999. All rights reserved. CLIFFORD® from CLIFFORD GETS A JOB by Norman Bridwell. Copyright © 1965 by Norman Bridwell. Reprinted by permission. CLIFFORD is a registered trademark of Norman Bridwell. JULIAN illustration from cover of MORE STORIES JULIAN TELLS by Ann Cameron. Illustration copyright © 1986 by Ann Strugnell. Reprinted by permission of Alfred A. Knopf, Inc. KERMIT: Kermit the Frog is copyrighted and used by special permission of Jim Henson Productions. LASSIE photograph by Daniel R. Westergren © National Geographic Society. Used by permission. MS. FRIZZLE illustration copyright © 1994 by Bruce Degen. Reprinted by permission.

"The Three Little Javelinas" from THE THREE LITTLE JAVELINAS by Susan Lowell, illustrated by Jim Harris. Text copyright © 1992 by Susan Lowell. Illustrations copyright © 1992 by Jim Harris. Published by Northland Publishing, Flagstaff, Arizona. Used by permission.

"Saguaro" from CACTUS POEMS by Frank Asch. Copyright © 1998 by Frank Asch. Reprinted by permission of Harcourt Brace & Company.

"Crossing the Creek" from LITTLE HOUSE ON THE PRAIRIE by Laura Ingalls Wilder. Text copyright © 1935 by Laura Ingalls Wilder, copyright renewed © 1963 by Roger L. MacBride. Illustrations copyright © 1953 by Garth Williams, renewed 1981 by Garth Williams. Reprinted with permission of HarperCollins Children's Books, a division of HarperCollins Publishers. "Little House" is a registered trademark of HarperCollins Publishers, Inc.

Selection from SEARCHING FOR LAURA INGALLS: A READER'S JOURNEY by Kathryn Lasky and Meribah Knight, photographs by Christopher G. Knight. Text copyright © 1993 by Kathryn Lasky and Meribah Knight. Photographs copyright © 1993 by Christopher G. Knight. Reprinted by permission of Simon & Schuster Books for Young Readers, an imprint of Simon & Schuster Children's Publishing Division.

"Reviews by You" from *Storyworks* magazine, September 1993. Copyright © 1993 by Scholastic Inc. Reprinted by permission.

Cover from LITTLE HOUSE IN THE BIG WOODS by Garth Williams. Illustrations copyright © 1953 and renewed © 1981 by Garth Williams. Published by HarperCollins Children's Books, a division of HarperCollins Publishers, Inc. "Little House®" is a registered trademark of HarperCollins Publishers, Inc.

"The Magic School Bus Hops Home" adaptation of production script by Jocelyn Stevenson based on THE MAGIC SCHOOL BUS book series by Joanna Cole and Bruce Degen. Copyright © 1993 by Scholastic Productions Inc. All rights reserved. THE MAGIC SCHOOL BUS and associated logos and designs are registered trademarks of Scholastic Inc. Used by permission.

"The Case of the Runaway Elephant" from ENCYCLOPEDIA BROWN LENDS A HAND by Donald J. Sobol, illustrated by Leonard Shortall. Text copyright © 1974 by Donald J. Sobol. Illustrations copyright © 1974 by Thomas Nelson, Inc. Used by permission of Lodestar Books, an affiliate of Dutton Children's Books, a division of Penguin Putnam Inc.

"I Spy: A Book of Picture Riddles" from I SPY: A BOOK OF PICTURE RIDDLES, photographs by Walter Wick, riddles by Jean Marzollo. Text copyright © 1992 by Jean Marzollo, photographs copyright © 1992 by Walter Wick. Reprinted by permission of Scholastic Inc. I SPY FANTASY: A BOOK OF PICTURE RIDDLES photographs by Walter Wick, riddles by Jean Marzollo. Text copyright © 1994 by Jean Marzollo, photographs copyright © 1994 by Walter Wick. Reprinted by permission of Scholastic Inc.

"Jessi's Baby-sitter" from THE BABY-SITTERS CLUB # 36: JESSIE'S BABY-SITTER by Ann M. Martin. Text copyright © 1994 by Ann M. Martin. THE BABY-SITTERS CLUB and APPLE PAPERBACKS are registered trademarks of Scholastic Inc.

A Century of Hits: PETER RABBIT: Illustration from THE TALE OF PETER RABBIT by Beatrix Potter. Copyright © 1902, 1987 by Frederick Warne & Co. Used by permission. BOXCAR CHILDREN: Cover illustration from THE MYSTERY OF THE HIDDEN PAINTING by Gertrude Chandler Warner. Cover illustration copyright © 1993 by Scholastic Inc. Reprinted by permission. THE BOXCAR CHILDREN is a registered trademark of Albert Whitman & Company. BABAR: Illustration from THE STORY OF BABAR by Jean de Brunhoff. Copyright © 1962 by Random House, Inc. Reprinted by permission of Random House, Inc. BATMAN image property of DC Comics. Used by permission. Batman is a trademark of DC Comics copyright © 1999. All rights reserved. MADELINE: Illustration from MADELINE AND THE GYPSY by Ludwig Bemelmans. Copyright © 1958, 1959 by Ludwig Bemelmans, renewed copyright © 1986, 1987 by Madeline Bemelmans and Barbara Bemelmans. Used by permission of Penguin Putnam Inc. LASSIE: Photograph by Daniel R. Westergren © National Geographic Society. Used by permission. CHARLIE BROWN: Copyright © 1950 United Feature Syndicate, Inc. Used by permission. RAMONA: Illustration from RAMONA QUIMBY, AGE 8 by Beverly Cleary, illustrated by Alan Tiegreen. Copyright © 1981 by Beverly Cleary. Used by permission of William Morrow Junior Books, a division of William Morrow & Company, Inc. CLIFFORD® from CLIFFORD GETS A JOB by Norman Bridwell. Copyright © 1965 by Norman Bridwell. Reprinted by permission. CLIFFORD is a registered trademark of Norman Bridwell. AMELIA BEDELIA: character image from one illustration from PLAY BALL, AMELIA BEDELIA by Peggy Parish, illustration by Wallace Tripp. Illustrations copyright © 1972 by Wallace Tripp. Reprinted by permission of HarperCollins Publishers. ENCYCLOPEDIA BROWN from ENCYCLOPEDIA BROWN: BOY DETECTIVE by Donald J. Sobol, illustrated by Leonard Shortall. Illustrations copyright © 1974 by Thomas Nelson, Inc. Used by permission of Lodestar Books, an affiliate of Dutton Children's Books, a division of Penguin Putnam Inc. KERMIT: Kermit the Frog is copyrighted and used by special permission of Jim Henson Productions. CHAPULIN COLORADO: Chapulin Colorado used by permission of Televisa, Mexico. JULIAN: Cover illustration from cover of MORE STORIES JULIAN TELLS by Ann Cameron. Illustration copyright © 1986 by Ann Strugnell. Reprinted by permission of Alfred A. Knopf, Inc. CARMEN SANDIEGO: Where in the World is Carmen Sandiego?® is based on the computer games from Brøderbund Software, Inc. WHERE IN THE WORLD IS CARMEN SANDIEGO?® CARMEN SANDIGO™ and the logo design are trademarks of Brøderbund Software, Inc. Used with permission. MS. FRIZZLE from THE MAGIC SCHOOL BUS book series by Joanna Cole and Bruce Degen. Copyright © 1993 by Scholastic Productions Inc. All rights reserved. Used by permission. IKTOMI: Illustration from IKTOMI AND THE BERRIES by Paul Goble. Copyright © 1989 by Paul Goble. Used by permission of Orchard Books, New York. ANIMORPHS: From ANIMORPHS: THE ENCOUNTER by K.A. Applegate, illustrations by David B. Mattingly. Copyright © 1996 by K.A. Applegate. Reprinted by permission of Scholastic Inc.

Photography and Illustration Credits